W9-DFC-916

THE JAPAN SYNDROME

THE JAPAN SYNDROME
Symptoms, Ailments, and Remedies

Jon Woronoff

Transaction Books
New Brunswick (U.S.A.) and Oxford (U.K.)

Published by Transaction, Inc., 1986.

Library of Congress Catalog Number: 85-20867
ISBN: 0-88738-090-5 (cloth)
Printed in the United States of America

Library of Congress Cataloging in Publication Data

Woronoff, Jon.
The Japan syndrome.

Bibliography: p.
Includes index.
1. Japan—Economic conditions—1945- .
2. Japan—Industries—1945- . I. Title.
HC462.9.W666 1986 330.952.'04 85-20867
ISBN 0-88738-090-5

Contents

Foreword

Ever since my first book on Japan was published in 1979, with the provocative and premonitory title of "Japan: The Coming Economic Crisis," I have been known as one of the strongest critics of Japan. Sad to say, I stood out more conspicuously because there were so few other critics around. This is a role I have not regretted, or I would not have adopted it. But the time has come to make somewhat of a break with the past.

By this, I do not mean that I will stop criticizing. Anyone familiar with the working of Japan's society, economy, and politics knows that there are vast numbers of things that are done so poorly that any other country would be ashamed of them. Other things are done reasonably well but could benefit from improvement. This is certainly the basis of a critic's work.

This work is all the more important in Japan. For, unlike many other countries, there is very little room for criticism within the system. Those who belong to the group, whatever group, are constrained to go along with what is done with hardly a groan or a whimper, and certainly without indulging in open criticism or doing what in the West is known as "blowing the whistle." Thus, criticism can only come from those outside of the system.

Among them, one potential source is foreigners. Oddly enough, whereas Westerners have bitterly criticized just about every nation under the sun and most fiercely their own, they have apparently found little wrong with present-day Japan. Indeed, there is a thriving literature vaunting the merits and charms of Japanese society and praising the awesome power and efficiency of its economy. While many of these commentaries are misinformed, when not outright lies, the impression does arise that things are much better than is the case. This only confirms the deeper feelings of too many Japanese that they really are superior.

That makes criticism from a foreigner particularly valid, first as an outsider who is at least permitted to criticize, secondly to compensate for the fawning twaddle of the claque of Japanophiles. While it may appear unpleasant or improper for a foreigner to tell the Japanese what is wrong, that is not really the point. What is most important is whether the criticism is correct and justified and whether it is given in the hope that it may do some good. Those are the two basic principles that I have tried to follow throughout.

But the time has come to go a step further. In addition to criticizing what is wrong, it is necessary to suggest other ways of doing things and recommend how to solve pending problems. This I have admittedly not done enough in the past and I should now like to make up for that lack.

Thus, this book consists of two parts. First an analysis of the Japanese syndrome, showing what I regard as wrong. And even that part is a twist on my earlier criticism. I do not claim that the economy is basically weak or inefficient but rather lopsided, with some excellent and other dreadfully mediocre sectors. I do not insist that it is a bad or evil system, whatever that may mean, but that while it is extremely productive it is not very fruitful. The Japanese get precious little out of the incredible effort they put in. Further, the strong points and merits, which are essentially related to modern exporting sectors, are a bit pointless today when Japan's exports are so often rejected abroad. These nuances are crucial.

The second part, which is more novel, consists of a number of suggestions as to where improvements could be made, what other sectors might be developed to stimulate growth and how Japan could better adapt to the inevitable economic slowdown and meet emerging social problems. To call them proposals would be pretentious; to think of them as a coordinated plan simply absurd. But they are clearly elements which should be considered and integrated in whatever efforts are made to pull out of the impending crisis and break with the old and increasingly harmful economic syndrome.

Certainly, knowing Japan as well as I do, I do not expect this book to unleash a wave of reform or result in concrete actions, not for the moment at least. I do not expect the readers to turn a new page or politicians to mend their ways just because I say so. As a matter of fact, I am quite certain that Japan will continue operating as it has in the past until economic circumstances and external political pressures, plus some changing ideas and tastes within the country, move it in new directions.

Still, it is always good to know the alternatives and have a broader picture of the situation. The scenario indicated it not just an expression of my personal views or wishes but more a prolongation of many trends which have begun materializing or even surfaced more visibly. In this sense, it can tell the Japanese and others in which directions they will probably be moving whether they want to or not. Of course, should they decide to move there voluntarily or actually make a determined push, the results would come faster.

The original suggestion for this book came from Shozo Shimaya and Katsuyoshi Saito of Diamond Inc., one of Japan's leading publishers of literature on economics and business. It was an excellent idea and I am pleased they proposed it. I also wish to thank several well-known publications for allowing me to reprint portions of the book which already appeared with them as articles. They are *Asian Business*, *Oriental Economist*, *South China Morning Post* and *Mainichi Daily News*.

JON WORONOFF

PART ONE

SYMPTOMS

1
The Second Crisis

Japan, The Former Growth Champion

Ever since they were proclaimed No. 1 by some over-enthusiastic foreign "experts," the Japanese have tended to regard themselves as truly superior in the sole activity that concerns them much, namely economics. It is already tedious to hear politicians, officials and businessmen wax poetic about Japan's great economic prowess and how the people struggled to rebuild and upgrade the economy. This is inevitably followed by the story of how the Japanese, seemingly alone to do so, managed to overcome both oil shocks.

Certainly, the Japanese have a right to be proud of their achievements. But it is quite another thing to come to believe that one is truly better than most others even in the only sector where serious efforts are made. This is a question of comparison and it is always essential that the comparison be fair.

Naturally, since Japan has been striving to catch up with, and then pass the West, ever since Meiji days over a century ago, it is not surprising that most comparisons are made with Europe and America. Indeed, the Japanese take ill-concealed delight in showing how much better they are doing than their former tutors. The proof of it all is that economic growth has remained stronger over the past two or three decades than in any other advanced country.

A look at the statistics will show that this is correct. Japan's growth during the 1960s was just over 10% while that in Western countries, including the United States, Germany, France and Great Britain, varied between 3% and 5%. During the 1970s, which included two oil crises, Japan's growth was nearly 5% while that of the same Western countries was a mediocre 2% to 3%. It is perfectly clear that Japan was doing much better than they and continues thus in the 1980s.

The only hitch is that, as all Japanese know, the growth rates in the West fell not only due to the oil crisis but also foolish economic policies, mismanagement in business and nagging social problems. This whole complex of factors is often summed up as the "Western disease," which spread from England, to the continent, and finally the United States. By now, it is not unusual to think in terms of a decadent West.

However, if the West is so inefficient, uncompetitive and disorganized, what is the point to such comparisons? The best that could be proven is that Japan is better than a bunch of places whose economies are in serious trouble. There must be more purposeful ways of measuring Japan's success or lack thereof.

The most sensible one is to compare Japan's economic performance now to its previous ability to show how it has fared over these past few decades. When that is done, as must be obvious, the Japanese do not shape up as well.

As already mentioned, Japan's growth rate fell from over 10% in the 1960s to under 5% in the 1970s. This was an evident decline which the Japanese would do well to reflect on. It is ludicrous to talk of any special economic prowess or upgrading in an economy that slowed down so sharply. And it is plain silly to claim that it "overcame" two oil shocks. The sad fact of the matter is that the Japanese economy was grievously weakened during the 1970s and is just a shadow of its earlier self in the 1980s.

One could go even further, and this time in a different comparison with the West. The economies in America and Europe had not been as strong to begin with, only ranging from 3% to 5% in the 1960s. When they slipped to an average of 2% to 3% in the 1970s, and a bit lower in the early 1980s, this was just a moderate dip. Japan, however, dropped from over 10% to under 5%, which was a loss of more than 5% growth and a much more dramatic decline. Actually, this was one of the worst tumbles that occurred anywhere during that period.

Unfortunately, the Japanese are so obsessed with their ranking against the West that they tend to forget the existence of other parts of the world. Naturally, they feel superior to folks in Africa, Latin America and parts of Asia whose economies are in a mess. And they do

The miracle fades. Slipping from high growth to low growth.

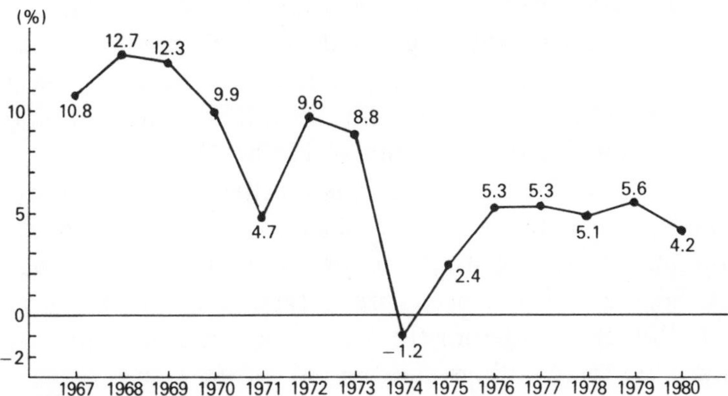

Credit: *Facts & Figures 1982*, Foreign Press Center, p. 43.

not think much more of the socialist bloc. But there is apparently no reason not to consider the situation in two groups of Asian countries which are its close neighbors and where economic performance has also been noteworthy.

The most notable, of course, are the "newly industrializing countries" of East Asia. There, economic growth was almost as high as in Japan during the 1960s, which was already quite an achievement. Much more striking is that, during the 1970s, they actually boosted their growth on the whole and were far more vigorous than Japan. The results were, very roughly, an impressive 7% for Taiwan, 8% for Singapore, 9% for Korea, and 10% for Hong Kong.

Somewhat further afield, in the ASEAN grouping, considerably more typical developing countries were proceeding reasonably well, although some have stumbled more recently. During the 1960s and 1970s, Indonesia, Philippines, Malaysia and Thailand were enjoying growth rates which ranged from 5% to 8% on the whole, actually doing somewhat better in the latter period than the former.

Compared to these two groups of countries, both of which faced pretty much the same difficulties, Japan's record does not look so good at all. Perhaps that is why it steadfastly avoids comparing itself to them and takes greater pleasure in showing how well it is doing by pointing to the flagging economies in the West.

Seen in such a light, Japan is hardly No. 1 any more. Maybe it was in the 1960s. But the 1970s left it greatly diminished and, during the 1980s, it may go the way of the West. Rather than praise themselves, and talk of some inherent superiority, it is about time the Japanese admitted their failings and figured out how to overcome them.

What Ever Happened To Productivity?

What ever happened to productivity? It used to be that you could hardly open a newspaper or turn on the television without being subjected to an appraisal of Japan's impressive performance. This has since been replaced by an uncomfortable silence in which the subject is rarely brought up. Only once in a while is there a rather brief and restrained mention.

The explanation for this is quite simple. Japan's productivity growth is no longer something to boast about. If anything, it *should* be a cause for concern. But the Japanese have adopted their customary attitude of simply forgetting about it so that they neither have to apologize nor bother themselves by seeking cures.

The facts of the situation are perfectly clear. During the 1950s and 1960s, Japan's productivity grew at an extraordinary pace, especially in manufacturing. Overall, it managed to maintain a growth rate of some 8.5% for over two decades and until the oil crisis in 1973. Then it dropped sharply to about 4% for the rest of the 1970s. In the early 1980s, it slipped further and periodically tumbled into a negative rate.

During the early period of rapid growth, the Japanese were extremely proud of their achievements and managed to attract worldwide attention. They even turned productivity into a religion of sorts, drawing disciples from numerous countries to admire the efficient factories and applaud the quality control circles. Even after the oil crisis, it was possible to put up a good show since growth was still twice as high as in the West. But there was no way of maintaining pretenses by the 1980s.

At present, Japan's productivity growth is not much better than that of other advanced nations and occasionally worse. Even the United States has thrown off its past sluggishness and attained more respectable levels. Certain European countries compare favorably over longer periods. If the classic chart of comparative productivity, the same old one the Japanese have been showing for decades, were to use 1970 (or 1980) as an index instead of 1955, Japan would not look particularly good. Indeed, if it added some successful developing countries like Korea, Taiwan, Hong Kong, Singapore and so on, it would look rather bad.

How can this amazing reversal be explained?

Actually, it is not that difficult. The explanation is perfectly natural and not really something to be ashamed of. Every developing country which launches into industrialization will show rapid growth in the early years, especially if it continues boosting output. And every industrialized country will reach a point where, no matter how hard it tries, it cannot expand productivity very much. This is all the more notable when output also slips.

Productivity is the relationship between production and the labor needed to obtain it. This production is measured in real terms, after correcting for inflation. The amount of labor can be taken in hours, as is usual in the West, or in days, the method adopted by Japan. Growth will come from increasing output, or decreasing labor, or both.

While the Japanese, in their zeal to impress, have laid exceptional stress on the human element, it is actually increases in capital or technology that make the biggest contribution. Even in Japan, they have accounted for well over three-quarters of any improvement. They boost production, using less labor, by increasing the amount of machinery used by each worker and expanding scale. They also introduce more efficient technologies and production techniques.

When this progress slows down, as indeed it must,

Productivity growth the way Japanese like to think of it . . . and how it really is.

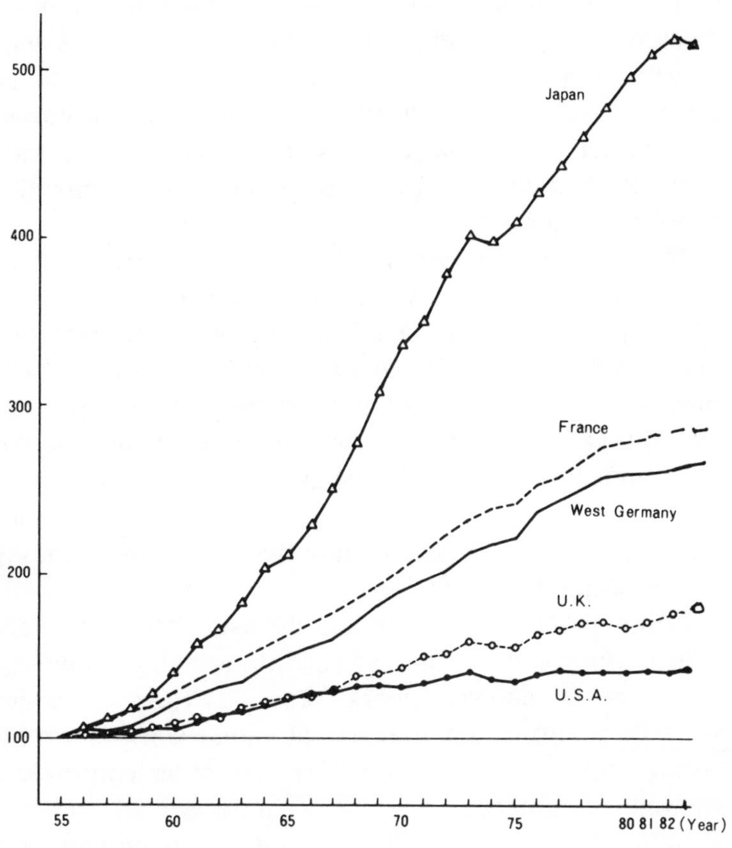

Average annual growth rate (%)

Year \ Country	U.S.A.	Japan	West Germany	France	U.K.
60～73	2.1	8.5	4.4	4.7	2.9
74～82	0.4	3.4	2.3	2.4	1.6

Credit: *White Paper on International Trade 1983*, MITI, p. 5.

productivity also slackens. The buildup of capital and technology in the earlier period was often to initiate branches that hardly existed while now it is just to replace machinery and therefore less urgent. Each increment nowadays brings forth a smaller increase in productivity since the prevailing levels are already so high. Moreover, it is harder to add more machinery or technology with production stagnant, interest rates high, and companies short of funds.

There are also other causes for stifling productivity which, although roundly condemned abroad, are scarcely mentioned in Japan. One is government "interference" and red tape arising from new regulations. While less prominent, there have been more regulations on what can and cannot be done, often to protect safety or the environment. Anti-pollution equipment is very expensive. And higher taxes dampen the incentives to invest in more plant and equipment even while they withdraw some of the essential funds.

Coming now to the human element, it is extremely delicate to argue that maybe something has gone wrong with Japan's renowned work force. But there are polite ways of pointing out that not as much work is wrung from it any more. It is obvious that older employees, as well as numerous middle-aged housewives, will not slave away as energetically as masses of young men and women. There has also been a shift from blue-collar to white-collar jobs, with the latter being considerably harder to supervise. And there is probably a bit more laziness and loafing, although it is carefully hidden.

But there are other causes related to the labor force which are not really its fault. When production stagnates, and factories work under capacity, it is unavoidable that the same work force will produce somewhat less. It takes time to cut back, especially in Japan, and this may not be done if it is assumed that business will pick up soon. In addition, when measuring labor by days (and not hours) worked, Japan's productivity is more seriously diminished by a fall in overtime.

These are the basic factors that have slowed down Japan's productivity growth. They are exactly the same factors that slowed down productivity growth in the West before it. And they are the self-same factors that will slow down productivity growth in the newly industrializing countries one day. There is nothing to be ashamed of aside from having boasted too loudly in the past and looking exceptionally bad when the inevitable occurs.

But there are a few other things Japan might consider now that productivity growth is not so easy to come by. These are also things which were glossed over, or concealed, in the past.

One is that it has consistently concentrated on productivity in manufacturing. That is where it was performing best and where it appeared as No. 1. But it was not doing anywhere near as well in other sectors, either agriculture or mining, on one side, or distribution, services and government, on the other. When its overall productivity growth, or even its non-farm productivity growth, are compared to those in other advanced nations, its performance was considerably less praiseworthy.

This is increasingly important now that industrial production has peaked in many branches and the tertiary sector is called on to play a more significant role. Productivity everywhere tends to accelerate with a shift from the primary to the secondary (manufacturing) sector, as it did in Japan. It also tends to decelerate with the shift from manufacturing to services, as has already begun.

There was also a deceitful propensity to stress productivity growth as opposed to the actual level attained. Naturally, Japan wanted to show how rapidly it was

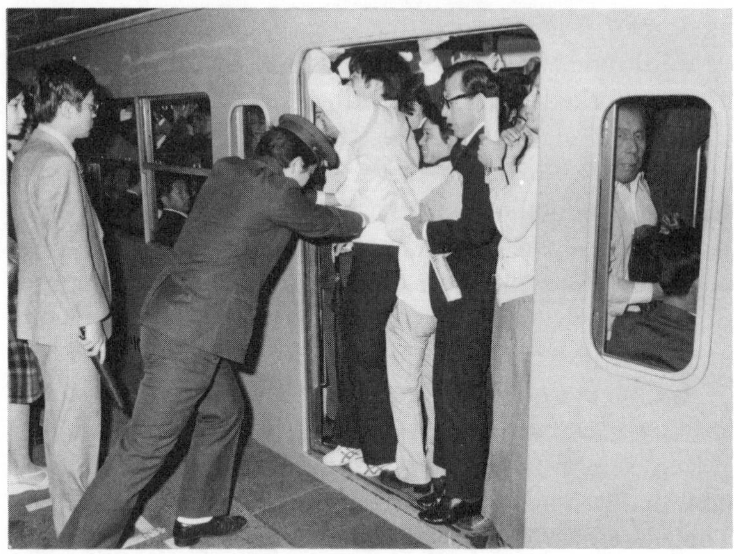

Enhancing productivity of the subways. Still champions here.

Credit: Foreign Press Center/Kyodo

catching up. But this created serious misconceptions among foreigners as well as in the minds of its own people (which was more dangerous) that Japan was already No. 1 there. It most definitely was not. For any number of products, it still falls behind the United States, Germany and some others.

Last, but assuredly not least, the stress on productivity led the Japanese to assume that it was the key to competitive strength. They ignored other factors, much to their detriment. Sales price, which is crucial in determining whether goods sell, depends not only on productivity. It is also a function of the cost of labor and equipment, the efficiency of transport and distribution, the price of energy and raw materials, and the level of the exchange rate. While Japan has done reasonably well on the former, the latter have repeatedly worked against it.

Transforming productivity into a religion, and making a fetish of the peerless Japanese worker, was perhaps understandable given the nature of Japanese society. But it has not helped. It has not forestalled the decline of both. Nor has it left room for more rational thinking about these important matters.

The (Far From) Rich Japanese

In their blind race to catch up with the West, the Japanese are not only eager to produce or sell as much. Quite naturally, they also want to earn comparable amounts and use their assets to create a better life for themselves. Thus, they are keenly interested in knowing how their income level compares to that of Westerners, a matter that is periodically discussed in government white papers or taken up by the media each time some new milestone is passed.

About a decade ago, the Japanese were pleased to learn that their income level was already higher than those of more peripheral European countries like Portugal, Spain or Greece. Not long after, they were closing in on the British and, a few years ago, they passed the French in earning capacity. Now they are finally drawing abreast of the front runners who once seemed unapproachable. By 1990, or so a recent study claims, the average Japanese should be earning more than the average American.

One would think that, with all this material progress, Japan would be a very affluent nation with people leading a life of ease and comfort. Indeed, that is the common impression abroad. But it is not quite as widely shared in Japan itself.

The big trouble with these statistics, which seem to prove something but really don't, is that they are nominal figures. It is just a matter of paper earnings and has little bearing on people's actual lifestyles. In order to know how well the Japanese are really doing, it is necessary to consider what they can buy with incomes that are increasingly among the highest in the world.

No sooner does one convert some francs, or pounds, or dollars into yen and attempt to buy something than it becomes painfully clear that the Japanese cannot get quite as far with their money as was thought. This bitter experience is made considerably more often than the pleasant surprise that one can actually get a good deal by using yen in Japan.

Among the most important daily necessities are food and drink. Due to an inefficient agricultural sector, and restrictions on imports, such common products as fruits, vegetables and meat turn out to be exceedingly expensive. Even rice costs more than in other countries where it is a staple. Milk is dear and alcoholic beverages even more so. This means that the average Japanese must either spend more money to eat or eat less.

Clothing is somewhat better because much of it is mass produced. Due to high wages, tailor-made clothing would be almost inaccessible. But even the standard ready-made garments are not as advantageous as in Europe and America these days because, once again, cheap imports are blocked.

The same applies to standard consumer goods like tape recorders, televisions or household appliances. Although so much of this is made-in-Japan, it seems that the goods are actually sold for a bit less abroad. That is because the Japanese makers control their home market and do not let in yet cheaper East Asian articles. Automobiles, at least, are good and no more costly . . . as long as you don't insist on a foreign car.

Given the small distances in Japan, it might be assumed that telecommunications and travel would be relatively cheap. True, local phone calls are reasonable. But calls outside of the city or, heaven forbid, abroad, can be pretty stiff. The same applies for postage. Commuter trains, local subways and taxies are no bargain. And it often costs less to fly to another country than from one Japanese city to another.

Essential utilities, like gas and electricity, are comparatively expensive. The same can be said for gasoline for the car.

But the real burden is housing. The Japanese pay about one-and-a-half times as much as Europeans and twice as much as Americans or Australians for the same type of house on an equally large plot of land . . . if they can afford it. In most cases, however, they make do with a much smaller house, rather poorly constructed, on a minute space with barely enough room to park the car and grow a few shrubs. In addition, they have the disadvantage of living as much as an hour or more commuting distance from work.

When it comes to amenities, it is no longer a question of cost but availability. While just about all households boast tap water by now, only half have flush toilets and a bit more than a quarter enjoy proper sewage. In most suburban districts, if that is what they can be called, there is a shortage of paved roads, sidewalks, parks and cultural facilities. This is obviously not the much vaunted, but not yet created, Japanese "garden city."

However, in life, it is not only concrete things which count. It is also necessary to consider some impalpables that make life truly worth living.

One of them is leisure. In order to earn their income, such as it is, most Europeans and Americans work some 250 to 400 hours less than the Japanese. This gives them more leisure in the form of weekends, holidays and

How is your livelihood now compared with a year ago?
More worse than better.

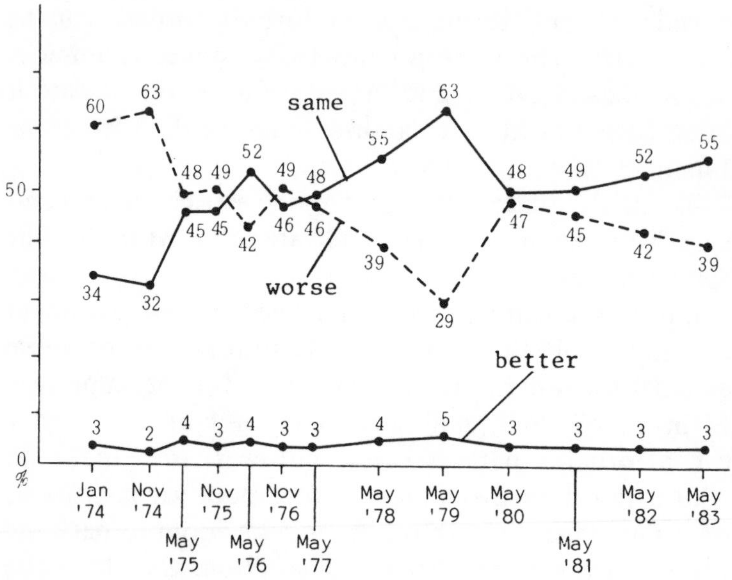

Source: *Survey on People's Living*, Prime Minister's Office, September 1983.

especially longer vacations. In fact, one of the greatest social gains has been to extend summer (and winter) vacations to three, four or five weeks.

In Japan, employees still work over 250 days a year. Only a minority are free for the whole weekend. Although they now have a legal right to over two weeks paid leave, most of them only take one week and "voluntarily" return the rest to the company. Overtime work is frequent. And socializing outside of working hours is almost obligatory. What is most surprising is that, despite gradually rising wages, there has hardly been any improvement in working time.

When it comes to security, the Japanese are still in a rather vulnerable position. Much is made of their abundant savings. But, after deducting debts, the average family only has about the equivalent of one year's earnings to fall back on. To this may be added two, or at most three, years allowance on retirement from the company. Then there is social security. However, with the major schemes dreadfully underfunded and increasingly cut back, it would not be very realistic to count on a steady or adequate income.

This means that even if the Japanese catch up with the Americans, and indeed, even if they become the best paid workers in the world, there is no reason to assume that they will enjoy a particularly affluent, agreeable or carefree existence.

Creating Social Insecurity

The Japanese have a very enviable reputation of looking into the future and preparing for it well in advance. They are also known far and wide for their respect of elders, sense of family, and social cohesion. Under such circumstances, one would assume that the difficulties other countries have faced in caring for the aged will not occur in Japan.

Yet, anyone who looks at what should be the main cornerstone of any such policy—social security—will find a situation that is in some ways disconcerting, in others simply disastrous.

So far, there has not been much trouble in caring for the aged because there are so few. Japan's was a very young society after the war and it has taken people time to grow up. It is only now that large numbers of old people exist and have to be looked after. But the situation is still not as advanced as elsewhere and those benefiting from social security are rather few.

However, it is already known that Japan's society is

aging at an exceptional rate. In fact, average life expectancy for men has reached 74 and, for women, an extraordinary 80 years. By the year 2020, it is reckoned that Japan will have the largest proportion of old people anywhere in the world.

This is bound to have its effect on social security as well as fewer people proportionately are paying premiums into the fund and more people proportionately are deriving benefits of one sort or another. At the present time roughly one old person is supported by twelve workers. In about thirty years, one old person will only be supported by three workers.

When that time comes, according to all authorities, the social security and welfare pension systems of the nation will be . . . bankrupt. Actually, they should be approaching insolvency at a much earlier stage and may even get into unsurmountable difficulties within the 1980s unless something drastic is done.

Just how serious the situation is can be readily gathered from a recent report of the Federation of Employers Associations (Nikkeiren) which deals with such matters as remuneration and working conditions on behalf of the Japanese business community.

By the year 2010, the financial situation of the various pension funds will be such the amount of benefits would have to be decreased to one fourth the present level or, alternatively, the premiums would have to be quadrupled.

Neither seems particularly appealing, or indeed, feasible. The present level of benefits is a barely acceptable one of about 40% of wages and, with savings and other sources of income, it is hard enough for most people to get by. It is impossible to conceive of any Japanese surviving on benefits that represent a mere 10% of wages.

Presently, the Japanese are paying in about 10% of their wages to the pension funds, evenly divided between employee and employer premiums. That is about half the level of some advanced industrial countries like Germany or Sweden and, by making a major effort, Japan could reach a level of 20% as well. But nobody expects premiums to become 40% of wages.

Thus, even the best possible scenario is none too good. That would be a doubling of premiums and halving of benefits. Life would be considerably leaner while one is young and paying premiums. But older people would at least have the equivalent of 20% of wages to fall back on. Still, this would imply a very frugal and almost marginal existence for those who did not have additional sources of income.

Given this preoccupying situation, it would be expected that the government is tackling the problem with the same vigor as other advanced countries, if not more. Instead,

Hospitals, the primary refuge for elderly people.

Credit: Foreign Press Center/Kyodo

what one finds is the complete opposite. Rather than reconstructing it, the rather flimsy system is being gradually dismantled.

The top priority of the Japanese government at present is implementation of a policy of administrative reform. No matter what that may sound like, what the policy aims at is summed up repeatedly as "balancing a sorely deficitary budget without new taxation."

One of the few ways ingenious politicians have found of doing so is to lop off some of the few social frills the average person enjoys. This has included bits of the national health insurance scheme, social security and welfare, and also education. There is no intention whatsoever of letting this policy be sidetracked by such needs as more social security in the future and thus the issue is basically suppressed.

The government's position is not only supported by business circles, they are the ones which imposed the administrative reform in order to escape tax increases. In such a mood, it would be unrealistic to expect the companies to either improve their own pension schemes or contribute more to the national social security system.

Even the opposition parties, including socialist and communist wings, have failed to make social security, health insurance, welfare or care for the aged effective issues. Trade unions are more concerned about their members' present earnings than their future well-being. As a matter of fact, there is no solid support in any major institution and old people have failed to organize in their own interest.

As for the bureaucrats, who are supposedly working behind the scenes to see that things run smoothly, they have more or less abandoned their efforts. The Finance and Welfare Ministries periodically issue reports demonstrating the precarious financial state of the various schemes and explaining that they will collapse if nothing is done. But they do not push very hard for action.

What will happen to Japan if this attitude continues, as it probably will at least for the forseeable future, and the necessary funds are not put aside on time?

That is easy enough to imagine. The elderly will be condemned to a lifestyle that will contrast sharply and unfavorably with that of their counterparts in more enlightened nations and with their fellow citizens who are still working.

Living costs in Japan are very high. While over half the people own their own housing, the remainder will need money to cover housing as well as food and clothing. There is no reason to expect that the amount of social security or other benefits will cover even that and there are virtually millions of old people who will be living close to subsistence level.

True, the Japanese are renowned as great savers. However, even their savings only amount to three or four years worth of wages and this would just improve their living standards slightly. On the other hand, public charity is extremely sparse and private charity begins—and ends—at home.

Most Japanese will thus be thrust upon their families and their children and probably grandchildren will have to help out. While that is the good old Japanese way, and sufficed in the past, it will not do in the future. Families are looser than before and many children are not that loving. Even if they were, they do not have much spare money and live in tiny dwellings with little room for others.

Moreover, with a life expectancy that will revolve around 80, it must be assumed that millions will be senile, sick or bedridden. They will need professional medical and nursing care and trained social workers or other personnel. The costs will far exceed anyone's capacity as an individual.

There is one last possibility, which Nikkeiren and some politicians are already considering. People could be encouraged to work longer. Instead of retiring from a long enough career at 55 or 60, as is presently the case, they could continue until 65 or 70. But it is obvious that many workers will not be healthy enough to carry on in any worthwhile capacity. And, with unemployment spreading even now, there is no reason to assume that there will be jobs for them.

Thus, by any criteria, the situation is lamentable already and becoming more alarming from year to year. Yet, nothing is being done to prevent the inevitable crisis and to fulfill the pledges that have been repeatedly made of a decent retired life for those who helped build the economy. The 21st century, broadly heralded as a heaven on earth for the Japanese, may be a hell of sorts for a large portion of the population.

PART TWO

AILMENTS

2
The "Sunset" Industries

Which Way Industry?

There is scarcely an economy which has received more coverage in the media than Japan's. Hardly a week goes by that someone does not discover a new industrial revolution or herald the coming of a promising new product. The air is full of catch-phrases like knowledge-intensive industry, the information age, the mechatronics revolution. Graphs show how the production of semiconductors, video tape recorders, computers, robots, and so on rise rapidly upward.

Yet, much of this information has led not to a better understanding of the Japanese economy but rather a total misunderstanding of its present situation and forseeable progress. The coverage has been almost systematically biased toward the more spectacular aspects and the more stunning successes. For this reason alone, it is highly misleading. To balance the picture it is necessary to think more of other sectors which have long since ceased their rapid growth and either matured or become stagnant. Nor can one neglect those which have already entered a decline.

Oddly enough, to know that such other sectors exist one need merely think back to the "miracles" of yore, the sectors and products that were touted by the press only a few years ago like petrochemicals and shipbuilding. Or, if you have a particularly good memory, such old favorities as textiles, footwear or toys. Just like any other country, Japan has worked its way through a whole series of products and some of them are no longer what they used to be. Its economy is mortal and it becomes harder to grow as the years go by.

Thus, to evaluate Japan's present situation and make any worthwhile forecasts of the future, it is necessary to adopt a much more balanced approach considering three categories of industries: growth sectors, mature sectors, and declining sectors. The purpose is not to praise or compliment one and condemn or criticize the other, but to see how they balance out. For Japan to keep growing, it is necessary for the new sectors to more than compensate for any weaknesses in the mature or older ones.

It is not enough for a new product to incorporate a brilliantly innovative technology or result from a production breakthrough that is unheard of elsewhere. It must also make a major contribution to the nation's economic strength. One way of doing so is to add to gross national product. Unfortunately, no matter how exciting some of the new technologies and how extraordinary some of the new products may be, they will remain out of reach for the vast public unless and until prices can be brought down substantially. This implies a long time lag from the laboratory to the mass market. Even then, some of the products will simply not result in large sales.

And, even if the sales are quite considerable, it must be remembered that many of the new products are merely replacing old ones. Just as color television stunted the growth of black-and-white sets, video tape recorders have been hurting sales of movie cameras and Sony's MAVICA will cut into the market for conventional cameras. The new materials like ceramics or titanium will only succeed once they replace plastics or other metals, as once synthetic fibers drove out natural ones. To evaluate the real contribution to gross national product one cannot simply indicate how much the new products may earn, as is usually done. You must also subtract the amount of sales that will be lost by older ones.

This approach helps overcome the misleading image one repeatedly gets from learning that some smashing new product, only a few years old, has managed to boost sales by a fabulous percentage or even double exports several years running. There is nothing so extraordinary about the rapid growth of a new product because that is always measured on a very small base. To give such a success, impressive as it may be, its true proportions, it is necessary to remember that a much smaller decline of an older industry can have a far greater impact on the economy. The older industries have already reached a relatively high level of turnover and, on this much bigger base, even a rather modest decrease can wipe out the gains of a spectacular rise elsewhere.

It will thus not be so simple to find enough new products to replace the old ones and maintain a growing level of affluence. It will be even harder to handle the employment aspects of this transition. Most of the new industries are highly capital-intensive and use relatively little labor. Most of the declining industries, to the contrary, employ large amounts of labor. This means that it will take a truly impressive increase in the growth industries to generate enough jobs to absorb workers who are already in, or would normally have entered, the more backward sectors.

Seen in this light, Japan is not quite in the enviable situation it is pictured in. Even if it has been more successful in opening up new sectors and has shown an unexpected ability at innovation, as opposed to imitation, there is no guarantee that it can keep ahead of the game. It will take much more new to replace the old, much more gains to compensate for the losses, much more ingenuity and much more luck than people think. This must be obvious to any lucid observer who has seen the economy slow down steadily during the 1970s. The 1980s will not be easier; they will be the most formidable challenge yet!

Industries At Their Peak

The Japanese economy is based on a number of mature industries which have grown over the years and now provide the bulk of its manufacturing production and an even larger share of its exports. These are the mainstays of the economy and as long as they remain sound there should be little trouble. Among them are products which have gained a worldwide reputation such as ships, automobiles, machinery, electronics and, the foundation of it all, steel.

The Japanese steel industry is doubtlessly the most efficient in the world and it is still highly competitive on price. That explains why it has been growing for such a long time, dipping just after the oil crisis, but picking up again thereafter. At present, the production level is around 100 million tons, which actually puts it ahead of the United States in most years. For exports, no other country even comes close. Yet, due to the worldwide recession and a sluggishness at home, the period of growth seems to be coming to an end.

It was cheap and strong steel that made it possible for Japan to produce ships of unmatched quality. When the shipbuilders rationalized production and introduced useful innovations (including better equipment and techniques as well as larger and more versatile ships), they found it easy to conquer much of the market. Ship production rose sharply until the oil crisis, when it collapsed. The fault was expensive oil and not Japanese workmanship. So, once the industry revived, the Japanese again claimed the lion's share of the market, but of a market that was considerably smaller. Still, for some time to come the shipyards should be working at close to present capacity.

The unpleasant slump in shipbuilding hardly affected the economy since the production of motor vehicles grew so quickly during the past decade. In a sort of poetic justice, this was thanks to—and not despite—the oil crisis. Japanese manufacturers had been specializing in small, fuel-efficient vehicles such as were essential for this crowded, resource poor country. When the oil price went wild after 1973, and again in 1979, Japanese cars, trucks, and motorcycles swallowed increasing shares of the world market.

In order to industrialize, and to make better products, the machinery industry developed rapidly and attained an unrivalled sophistication. After copying foreign samples for a while, local companies gradually showed just how inventive they could be. Most of the machinery became increasingly precise and also cheaper. More significant, the manufacturers soon took advantage of computers to introduce numerically controlled machine tools and machining centers as well as other automatic machinery. Now they have completed the circle by introducing robots. So, while textile machinery or simpler tools declined, there was always something new to offer the clients. Lately this has meant not only individual units but whole systems and on occasion vast turnkey factories.

Another industry that has kept abreast of the times

is electrical apparatus and electronics, both consumer and industrial. It did not take Japanese manufacturers long to produce the standard range of household appliances as well as washing machines and refrigerators. Nor was there any delay in introducing radios and TVs and then pushing ahead to tape recorders, calculators and VTRs. Thousands of different types of electrical machinery are also produced. As one kind lost popularity it was usually replaced not by another but several others. This has made electrical goods and electronics both a mainstay and a growth industry.

There are many other sectors that have reached a high degree of maturity as concerns quality of the product and the ability of the manufacturers. Among them are basic chemicals, office machinery, printing equipment, optical goods and watches. But it is more significant to note that the biggest industry is also in this category,

How much further can rationalization go?

Credit: Nippon Kokan

namely construction. This developed along various lines. One is basic infrastructure such as roads, bridges, and tunnels. Another is plant construction to provide suitable facilities for the widening circles of industries. And finally housing construction, to offer the Japanese people somewhat better and slightly larger accomodations.

The word maturity has a very nice ring to it. It makes one think of a high quality of workmanship, efficient production techniques, and strongly competitive products. It tends to involve a rather large and steady flow of goods. But we cannot forget that maturity can also imply the end to steady expansion and the onset of stability. This stability can then lead into stagnation and turn maturity into the peak of the growth process and the threshhold to decline.

These reflections are not made for purely philosophical reasons. Most of the industries referred to have actually passed, or are now coming close to, their peak in terms of production. Steel output has not grown noticeably of late and is not expected to expand much in the future either. Shipbuilding has stabilized at an impressive level when compared to other countries, but it is much lower than during the pre-oil crisis boom. For the first time, automobile production has reached a ceiling with stagnant demand at home and restrictions abroad. Growth of the machinery and electronics industries is somewhat slower. And construction has fallen recently.

This is not necessarily the beginning of the end, let alone the end of the road. Japan can continue depending on its mainstays and may develop a few more. But it cannot afford to forget that every industry reaches the point where it *must* stop growing. There will eventually be a saturation point for any product. The average person or family can only buy so many TVs, VTRs, calculators or cars. This point comes suddenly closer when there is a recession and money is tight. And, for overly successful exporters like Japan, it can be imposed by others in the form of trade barriers.

Industries On The Way Down

To read the many forecasts of the Japanese economy or the more lyric passages of the usual Japan supplements in the press, you would think that there were no declining industries in Japan. There is much talk of VTRs, computers, and robots. Little is said about less glamorous industries like plastics and footwear or even some of the earlier growth sectors like synthetic fibers and shipbuilding.

However, just because they are forgotten or brushed over does not mean that they do not exist. There is a large and growing contingent of weak industries which are not only losing market share but actually shrinking in absolute terms. Some lost their competitive edge and could no longer export. Others are being battered by imports. By now, several of them could be regarded not only as declining but severely ailing sectors.

One broad category includes a range of products characterized by rather backward technologies and distressingly labor-intensive methods. They are often just listed as "sundries" in the trade statistics: tableware, porcelain, wood products and furniture, lacquerware, etc. There are also larger sectors such as footwear and toys. Despite their present state, they were once flourishing sectors. Meanwhile they have been eclipsed by competition from the nearby industrializing countries.

More significant has been the gradual slippage of the textile industry. Raw and woven silk, which propelled Japan's first economic booms, was gradually phased out and has already become almost negligible. Cotton and other natural fibers actually reached their peak production before the war and stabilized at a somewhat lower level during the postwar period. Garments, due to the tremendous amount of labor involved, have done quite poorly of late and Taiwanese and Korean articles now prevail for many types. What saved the textile industry was synthetic fibers. Yet, even there production peaked in 1979 while exports remain erratic.

Although it is rarely mentioned as a declining industry, it must be remembered that the whole primary sector of agriculture has long been on the wane. Its share of gross national product dropped from above 10% in 1960 to below 5% in 1980. Moreover, the prices of local agricultural produce are so high by international standards that the present levels of production can only exist due to big tariff barriers and small quotas. Mining has all but ceased for most minerals. The attempt to revive coal mining recently may have received a death blow with the Yubari mine disaster (aside from the fact that costs were too high to begin with).

But it is not only farm produce that would be threatened if Japan were opened to trade. Processed foods are also very expensive due to the high cost of ingredients, most of which are imported or sold at inflated Japanese prices. At stake here are quite substantial enterprises producing ham and sausages, biscuits and confectionaries, frozen and canned foods, and beverages of all sorts. The many sugar refineries, which have already fallen on bad days, are symbolic of the state the industry could be in and may ultimately enter.

Aside from these older sectors, which have been facing difficulties for years and sometimes decades, there is a new group of problem industries which surfaced more recently. Their trouble can be traced to the oil crisis. One batch consists of products derived largely from petroleum, including some basic chemicals and petrochemicals. The high cost of naphtha used in Japan as opposed to cheaper natural gas used abroad has led to a slump for domestic production of ethylenes and propylenes. Other items which are hurt are plastics (and indirectly the vast range of products made from plastic) as well as chemical fertilizers. It might be added that most oil products have been selling so poorly since the huge price hikes that the oil companies themselves are hard pressed to get by.

The second batch of industries depends heavily on energy for processing. To this can be added the often increased costs of essential raw materials. Thus, for example, aluminum refining has been severely stricken by the high cost of electricity and imported bauxite, which make up about 75% of production costs. Japanese aluminum has been priced out of the market and the refiners had to reduce capacity by about half over the past three years. Similar difficulties afflict the copper, zinc and lead smelters. Fortunately, given the vast scale of steelmaking operations and rapid technological progress, this crucial industry has avoided becoming a casualty so far. The same cannot be said of pulp and paper, voracious consumers of energy and raw materials.

The foregoing progression is interesting in itself. Japan's economic development first arose out of light industry making use of surplus population, while agriculture sustained the nation. The later, postwar wave of development concentrated on what was lumped together as "heavy and chemical industries." Now all of them are in some trouble, both the old-fashioned labor-intensive sectors and the more modern capital and technology-intensive sectors. And this is occurring in a country where limited raw materials and high labor costs offer little inherent comparative advantage for many of the products its economy is rooted in.

For such reasons, it would be unwise to play down, let alone overlook, this phenomenon. The rot which has started in certain industries is bound to spread and it will not be so easy to help those sectors that can be saved while moving on to more promising ones. Moreover, the basic changes will have to be made from an increasingly shaky foundation.

Fattening Japan's Farmers

The Japanese farmers are in many ways like the celebrated Kobe cattle. There are relatively few of them and they are carefully looked after. They are stuffed with costly inputs and allowed to grow. When it comes to selling the beef, however, the price is so high that hardly anyone can afford it.

This conclusion becomes painfully evident when considering the economics of beef breeding in Japan. Most of the "ranches," if they can be called that, only have half-a-dozen head of cattle and a farmer with more than a dozen or so is a rarity. The cattle are kept in small sheds and have access to equally small pens for periodic exercise. Most of their time is spent being fattened.

Fattening, alas, consists only partly of having them graze and eat natural grass or being fed grass that is grown locally. The rest of the fodder is imported from the United States, which makes it very expensive. Since cattle are not very good converters, it takes a tremendous amount of feed to get a pound of meat.

The ultimate result is good—but terribly expensive—beef. The price differential is roughly 4:1, with Japanese meat costing four times as much as imported beef.

The situation is similar for just about every crop in Japan. Citrus fruit is also difficult to cultivate given the limited space. Mandarine oranges, the local type, are about three times as expensive as imported oranges. More exotic fruit like bananas, kiwi, or grapefruit can be four or five times more costly. Even vegetables are probably twice as dear.

Indeed, surprising as it may seem, even the staple crop of rice is grossly overpriced. Domestic rice costs about twice as much as American rice would cost, if it could be imported. In addition, since too much is usually produced, the excess must be stored at additional expense. And, in the attempt to replace rice with wheat, new subsidies became necessary for that crop.

This absurd price structure could only be maintained because the Japanese have painstakingly constructed a dense network of subsidies, import restrictions and price support. This was the handiwork of the ruling Liberal Democratic Party which depends heavily on the farm vote. But the farm lobby is much broader, including opposition parties as well. The actual measures were conceived by the Ministry of Agriculture which never tires of seeking new and varied ways of helping the farmer.

The methods used are multiple and often cumulative, since most Japanese farmers benefit from several. For rice, it is quite simple. The government buys the rice at higher rates, which are fixed politically each year, and then sells at a lower price to avoid the wrath of the average citizen. Since there is too much rice, however, the farmers are paid to take land out of rice production and go into something else. That is where things get really bad.

The areas toward which the farmers have been encouraged to move are even less productive normally, since the price differentials against imports are even greater. Thus, it became essential to block imports aside from modest quotas imposed by angry trading partners. In this case, rather than a subsidy from the government, supply is restricted so that the farmers can command a sufficiently high price directly from the consumers.

In addition to this, the farmers are given special loans by various government banks, usually with very low interest rates and long repayment, to purchase any equipment. There are masses of extension workers and specialized institutes to provide the knowhow. So entry into the new sector is facilitated by the authorities and the farmers are grateful enough to reelect them.

While not generally noticed, there is another group of beneficiaries from this scheme. The biggest winners are actually the distributors who monopolize imports and can sell them at two, three or four times the price they fetch abroad because of the artificially high prices in Japan. They can, and regularly do, make a killing.

The consequence, as shown by a recent study of the Forum for Policy Innovation, chaired by Professor Yasusuke Murakami of Tokyo University and Professor Chikashi Moriguchi of Kyoto University, is one of the highest price support levels in the advanced countries. According to them, only minute and mountainous Switzerland has a higher ratio. Japan, at 46, is well ahead of the European Community as a whole, at 26, or the United States, close to zero.

But this was not the most troubling conclusion. While the price support ratio was declining in all the other countries, in Japan it has continued rising, from a low 15 in 1955, to a moderate 29 in 1960, to a high 42 in 1970, and an exceptional 46 in 1983. Moreover, if the farmers, farm lobby and farm-related officials have their way, this could keep on indefinitely in the future making food costs even more exorbitant than today.

It is therefore obvious that care and protection of the agricultural sector is getting out of hand. The time has certainly come to start dismantling the price support system and imposing a bit more realism on the farmers and their backers. That will doubtlessly be painful, and will most assuredly be resisted by those concerned, but to do anything else would court disaster.

3
The Rat Race

The "Bicycle Economy"

The Japanese often refer to their economy as the "bicycle economy." What is meant by this is very graphic and almost poignant. A bicycle only stays erect as long as it is pedalled. The instant you stop pedalling, it falls down. The same would happen to its companies and the whole economy if people paused even briefly.

That is a rather odd analogy for the Japanese to make, or so most foreigners would think, since Japan's economy is regarded abroad as one of the most dynamic and aggressive. Yet, those are also aspects of a bicycle economy and, even though they appear as virtues, they can add to the sad fate of the bicyclists by making them pedal ever faster in order to keep moving.

What this means in practice is not hard to find. In fact, the same phenomenon arises in almost every sector of activity. The Japanese economy is based on scale, on ever increasing scale, making it possible to bring costs down more rapidly. But, as soon as production goes up and more articles have to be sold, it is not only costs which fall . . . so do prices and often profits.

This obeys the immutable law of supply and demand whereby, as soon as supply grows faster than demand, it is only possible to sell the goods for a somewhat lower price in order to coax new purchasers into the market. It is a law that the Japanese would not seem to be aware of, although it is taught widely in their business schools and is carefully observed in other capitalist countries.

In Japan, infractions of this law are not so simple to document for the very reason that the Japanese are so obsessed with increasing scale, production and market share that most of their statistics are issued in the form of quantity of sales rather than value. It is easy to know how many automobiles, or machine tools, or tons of steel the Japanese produced or exported in a given year. It is much harder to find out what they made from it.

Still, the situation of certain industries or certain companies is so shaky that it is obvious that even when they produce more they do not manage to earn more. In other cases, the quantity and sales trends are strikingly varied. Nevertheless, even here the primary goal remains to produce yet more in the vain hope that this time the extra production will bring in much needed extra earnings.

To show what this means, one can look at some sectors where the bicycle syndrome is most pronounced or where, through some oversight, both quantity and value statistics are available. They include waches, motorcycles and video tape recorders which are reasonably representative of Japanese products in general.

While Japanese watch and clock production has been rising for years, the value per unit has been falling as fast or faster. This is not surprising, since there was a tendency for cheaper digital watches to replace more costly mechanical ones. And one way of expanding production was to sell more in the cheaper categories. But that is not quite enough to to explain how the total sales value could fall by as much as 26% a year ago.

The real explanation is that the Japanese completely

forgot economic rationality and strongly boosted supply in the midst of a recession, at the very time that demand was drying up. They therefore heaped extra quantities of watches on the market and incited cutthroat competition to sell the existing stocks at any possible price.

This left the bicycle economy pedalling on air. Naturally, the bicyclists got into some trouble. Despite their huge size and apparent solidity, even companies like Citizen or Seiko were hurt by sluggish sales and Ricoh Watch made nasty losses. In fact, it was only able to survive because it was bailed out by the mother company and became a parts supplier for another watchmaker.

The value figures are not accessible for motorcycles, but the epic struggle between Yamaha and Honda is well-known. Yamaha decided a few years ago to pull ahead of Honda by bringing out many new models, expanding scale, cutting prices and selling more to win a bigger market share. Honda replied with a sudden burst of speed, turning out new models, at cheaper rates, and in larger quantities.

The result was a sudden glut of motorcycles on the world market. Actually, at the peak, there were reportedly one million unsold units in Japan, another million in Europe and yet another in the United States. That represents almost half of a normal year's production. With so much excess inventory, of course, prices had to be slashed and no one made much out of the adventure. The smaller makers, Yamaha, Suzuki and Kawasaki were badly hurt, but Honda was bruised as well.

Things haven't gone quite that far for video tape recorders, although the bicyclists are travelling at breakneck speed with little concern as to where they are heading. Back in 1975, only 119,000 VTRs were produced, by 1979, output had increased to 2,199,000, and in

1983 it was already 17,800,000. This was an absolutely incredible boost of 150 times which brought VTRs from a rarety to a common household gadget.

But a look at the value figures gives a considerably different impression of how well Japan did. Sales value rose from ¥25 billion in 1975 to ¥1,495 billion in 1983, an appreciable amount but only 60 times higher. This means that the unit value shriveled from ¥208,000 each to ¥85,000 each, which is not even a third the earlier level if one considers inflation.

Admittedly, part of this was due to the benefits of increased scale and mechanization, which made VTRs easier to produce. Part was also due to introducing cheaper models. But another share had less enviable causes. There were so many VTRs being produced that prices just collapsed and, when inventories built up,

Reporting for another hectic day in the city.

Credit: *Foreign Press Center/Kyodo*

already cheap VTRs were sold with an additional 20% or 30% discount.

Alas, the crucial set of figures is missing, namely what sort of profits the VTR makers got. But it can be assumed that they were not earning much and it should not be long before there is a major shakeout of the industry with the weaker producers falling by the wayside and even the supposedly "successful" ones making precious little out of a product that could have been a gold mine if they had bothered heeding the law of supply and demand.

Thus the bicycle economy rolls on with the bicyclists pedalling ever harder and progressing less rapidly than before. Their only chance of escaping this fate is to slow down a little, so that demand can catch up with supply and pull them forward. But they are afraid to pause lest they fall.

Japanese-Style Competition

In the press and even books about Japanese management, we read much about how the company is structured and coordinated but almost nothing about how it functions. It must be obvious even to the simple-minded that a company's purpose is not to create consensus among its own employees but to compete effectively in the market place.

In fact, an extraordinary urge for, and ability at, competing is one of the truly salient features of Japanese business. This is a competition which, be it mentioned in passing, is far more intense and destructive than can be found in most other countries. It frequently becomes so fierce that the Japanese have a disparaging term to refer to it, namely *"kato kyoso"* or excessive competition.

Obviously, the competitive struggles will take different

forms in different sectors and at different times, but there is an amazing similarity to the way Japanese companies act and interact. This has resulted in a standard scenario which is repeated time and again.

It usually starts when a large number of companies, acting almost in unison, decide that a given sector or product offers exceptional potential. This is not surprising since Japanese employees have a strong sense of rivalry, one which is consciously nurtured by management and directed against competing companies. They constantly try to keep up with, or pull ahead of, one another.

This creates a tremendous bandwagon effect which is quite capable of turning an initially dull sector into a growth industry almost overnight not because it is inherently that good but because none of the competitors can afford to stay out. If it does not materialize, they will all have made the same mistake. If it would result in pathbreaking innovations or popular products, they cannot afford to be left out.

Getting into the field is not terribly difficult for the relatively large Japanese companies, equipped with substantial production capacity and research staff, and able to draw on the support of the company bank. Most products, including the most novel, can usually be produced by using different methods and can be altered just enough to get around the patent or model protection. The true pioneers rarely have more than one or two years' headstart over the rest of the pack.

Thus, within an amazingly short time, there are not a few but literally dozens of companies doing, or trying to do, the same thing. This has happened for just about any and every product, bicycles, motorcycles, ships, radios, digital watches, household appliances and now solar installations, VTRs, robots, pharmaceuticals and genetic engineering.

Obviously, with so many companies creating new facilities and expanding capacity, there will quickly be overproduction and it will be necessary to fight hard to win new customers. The normal competition will be aggravated by the fact that the Japanese are not only trying to sell but win market share and drive their rivals out of the market.

The confrontation usually takes the form of price competition as companies try first to bring costs down by improving their production techniques or increasing their economies of scale. In so doing, also, they may have raised output to such an extent that the price will collapse anyway due to a sudden oversupply. This happened recently for the 64K RAM chips whose price plummeted to about a tenth of what it had been a year before.

Even when there are no natural economic causes for the fall in prices, it may arise from a deliberate strategy of undercutting the competitors. Prices will be brought down aggressively, not only to the break-even point but far below. Companies may have to take a loss of 10%, 20% or more, as has happened for ships, household appliances, or computers.

This is the first stage of *kato kyoso*. Naturally, among the mass of companies, some will be very weak or incompetent and should perhaps never have entered the field to begin with. Others, although good (often including the pioneers), may not have the financial backing. Thus, gradually, they will drop out and the ranks of producers will be thinned radically.

Of course, once the sector is more compact with fewer producers, the competition will let up and companies will try to replenish their funds and recoup their earlier losses. They will try to outdo one another more on quality or on service and shun price competition. In fact, if the field of contenders is narrow enough and the relations reasonably close, they may well jack the prices up to a level which more than compensates for their earlier sacrifices.

Over the years, as new models are introduced or new companies try to break into the sector, there can be similar competitive battles and price wars. Otherwise, things will be reasonably calm and the market share of each company will remain almost stationary. It is not until much later that the second major bout in the standard scenario takes place.

Somewhere along the line, for every product that exists, there must be a point when the market has become relatively saturated and starts shrinking. At that time, the various producers will again find themselves with excess capacity and stuck with machinery and personnel they cannot discard fast enough. Like it or not, they must produce and sell and, to do so, they must compete fiercely again.

This, too, has been a frequent phenomenon in the business scene. Indeed, the most severe cases of *kato kyoso* occur in the ailing industries like textiles, garments, pulp and paper, aluminum, and so on. But it is more deadly since it happens among companies that are themselves weakening and in sectors which the banks are less eager to shore up.

To put an end to the competition which, it is generally feared, would eventually be detrimental not only to the producers but the economy and nation as a whole, the Ministry of International Trade and Industry may intervene. When it does, it will usually propose the introduction of an anti-recession cartel which normally provides for an orderly reduction in capacity by all the producers. Quite frequently, it will also include arrangements for merging the smaller, weaker units into larger, more viable ones.

Thus, periods of fierce competition alternating with periods of passive coexistence or active collusion (which is not quite the same thing as harmony!) tend to typify the activities of many companies. Moreover, MITI's function as a referee and mediator in cases of *kato kyoso* is certainly just as important nowadays as its function of providing administrative guidance for growth used to be.

"Boomerangs" And "Doughnuts"

About ten years ago, Nippon Steel and a group of other companies won what they thought was a terrific deal. Korea had been planning to build a large integrated steelmill whose construction was first offered to a consortium of Western steelmakers. That arrangement never got off the ground due to unwillingness to provide sufficient credit. Then the Japanese stepped in and began supplying the plant and equipment, on good credit terms, for a first, second, third and fourth blast furnace.

Now that "terrific deal" has come back to haunt them. For, Pohang Iron and Steel Company is finally in a position to meet most of Korea's domestic requirements and Japanese steel exports were cut back correspondingly. They also face growing competition on third markets, especially in Southeast Asia but also the United States. Worse, Japan has begun importing Korean steel itself. When the new integrated mill is completed, Japanese exports to Korea should fall to about nothing and imports on its own market will grow from the present modest level.

This example vividly illustrates what the Japanese have

come to refer to as the "boomerang" effect. Japan ships plants and equipment abroad which in time become productive and replace its own exports. Then, as capacity expands and sophistication rises, these companies begin competing against Japanese products on third markets and even the home market. The brilliant idea of making some extra money by selling knowhow boomerangs back and hits Japan.

The Japanese probably deserve this. For they refused to believe that there could be any boomerang effect until it was flying at them. The logic behind many of these sales was that the technology and equipment were being sold to developing countries which, or so many Japanese believed, were so incompetent that they could not possibly use them properly and would thus remain inefficient and uncompetitive internationally.

This simplistic view was disproven in Pohang. The Koreans were extremely successful there. They are using excellent Japanese equipment in combination with highly trained and motivated local technicians and workers. This enables them to produce steel of the best quality and to do so more cheaply, since they make considerable savings on labor costs as well on land and amortization. They are competitive and can actually sell their steel for less than the Japanese.

If it were only the case of the Pohang steelmill, this would not be so serious. But Japan has been extremely active in promoting such projects around the world. In the steel sector alone, one can refer to several huge ventures. There is the Baoshan complex in China, two huge steelmills in Brazil, and smaller projects in Mexico, Egypt and the Middle East. Of course, although it did not participate, other plants in Latin America and Eastern Europe have exactly the same impact.

Similarly, if it were only the case of steel, then perhaps

the repeated blows from the boomerang could be endured. But this is not the only boomerang. There are many others.

Japanese companies also opened textile factories in many developing countries which were designed basically for domestic purposes. Later, under somewhat more pressure, they also set up synthetic fiber plants and, to obtain economies of scale, made them considerably larger. Now, many of these countries can supply their own goods which have replaced Japanese products. Worse, places like Korea, Taiwan, Hong Kong and other Asian countries, have used the Japanese investments or equipment as the basis for their own textile and fiber industries. For some time already, they have successfully invaded the international market and pushed back the Japanese for lower price and quality articles.

A similar progression took place for electronics. Much of the equipment in Asia was supplied by the Japanese, some of it for cash, the rest through investments and joint ventures. The result has been the rise of Asian electronics industries which have slowly but surely nibbled at Japan's earlier supremacy. They have nearly driven it out of the market for simple items like fans, radios, cassette recorders and black-and-white television and are chasing up for color television and video tape recorders.

While such dangers clearly existed for light industry, the Japanese were a bit foolhardy to assume that the trick could not be repeated in heavy and chemical industries as well. As demonstrated, even a product like steel was vulnerable. In addition, Ishikawajima-Harima Heavy Industries built huge shipyards in Brazil and Singapore which have eaten into Japan's own sales. And there is a welter of petrochemical plants of one sort or another underway or nearly completed. Only the one in Iran followed the "optimistic" scenario of being demolished before it could go into production. Others will soon be competing against Japanese products.

How could this happen? Part of the fault was wishful thinking, with the Japanese assuming they could always keep well in front of the pack. In many cases, they managed to remain one or two steps ahead of the newcomers. But this only enabled them to hold the top of the market for the most sophisticated goods. The rest of the market, often more than half, was lost to competitors who were put in business by the Japanese themselves.

The other aspect may be regarded as a form of greed. Having built up their own industries and expanded as much as possible, the Japanese companies were not willing to stop pressing for growth and concentrate on profits. When the only way to obtain growth was overseas investment and sales of plant and equipment, they took that path. Steel and textile companies set up special divisions to market knowhow. Plant and equipment makers launched aggressive campaigns. Engineering firms and trading companies organized vast turnkey projects. And the government and commercial banks stood by with easy credit.

Thus, sales of plant and equipment increased rapidly. Moreover, the divisions and companies selling them more often won out over those in the production and export divisions who warned of the dangers. And their cries of alarm were lost in the scramble of international bidding. The Japanese always worried that if they did not get the order it would go to a domestic competitor or the Americans and Europeans. So they actively created many of the boomerangs that would bombard them later.

While this process would seem unpleasant enough already, it unfortunately tied up with another that made the situation yet worse. This one is known as the "doughnut" phenomenon. It appears primarily in the sectors for processing raw materials and has resulted in a disappearance of productive activities in the center and their transfer out of the country.

The reasons vary. In some cases, it is clearly more rational to engage in processing of raw materials where they are found. If nothing else, it is simpler. And now some producer countries demand it. Thus, over the years the Japanese have been investing in the production of alumina which is then processed back home and, more recently, aluminum ingots which are imported and used for industrial purposes. This, of course, has had the effect of undermining the domestic smelters. A similar process is now occurring for copper, tin, lead, and so on.

A second impulse for ceasing local metal smelting and refining is the skyrocketing cost of energy, which is used in very large quantities. Some of the investments are made in areas which do not even possess raw materials but where electricity is cheap. This will explain the Asahan project in some ways, since the bauxite is taken from a far distant Indonesian island. Places where bauxite is close by are naturally more efficient and include the Amazon project in Brazil and several ventures in Australia, all with substantial Japanese participation.

A third reason for such projects is growing concern about pollution in Japan. It is therefore welcomed by the populace, and increasingly the government, that much of the preliminary and dirtier processing should take place abroad. This is probably the best explanation of Kawasaki's sintering plant in the Philippines. While it is disturbing the ecology of a beautiful area, it must be admitted that this is making some contribution to the Philippine economy . . . and hurting Japan's.

What is happening for metals can apply to many other products as well. One of them is paper and pulp. Paper-making requires huge supplies of wood, plenty of space, and lots of water. It uses rather simple technologies which are very polluting. So these operations have gradually been shifted to places like Canada and the United States where they already exist or to Brazil, thanks to another huge Japanese investment project. A side effect, of course, is that another domestic industry is being lost.

There are numerous other cases, including the processing of just about any agricultural raw material. There is no reason why the first steps in converting wood into plywood, jute into fiber, coffee beans into soluble coffee, rubber into latex, and so on should not be undertaken abroad. Often they are. Frequently with Japanese plant and equipment.

But the most striking case is petrochemicals and their many derivatives including plastics and synthetic fibers. The basic feedstock nowadays is naphtha . . . or natural gas. The naphtha is much more expensive in Japan than near the oil field. Thus, at present the United States and later the Arab countries, Indonesia or Mexico will be ruthlessly competitive and could wipe out Japanese exports and then take ever growing shares of its domestic market.

Associated natural gas is the bigger threat. Much of this was earlier flared off. Now more is being tapped directly for use in petrochemical production. The cost is much lower, to some it is regarded almost as "free" because otherwise it would be wasted. At any rate, by using it, countries with natural gas could produce goods that are much more competitive against anything the Japanese could make out of imported feedstocks.

In this connection, the cause was less any foolishness on the part of the Japanese than some unpleasant facts of economic life. Japan does not have any real comparative advantage for processing raw materials, and this includes even steel, aside from high technology. Other countries possess the raw materials, energy, and other inputs. The sources are close enough to avoid the costs and wastage of shipping. In addition, they often have more land and cheaper labor. When Japan sells them the missing link, namely its technology in the form of knowhow or plant and equipment, it is finished.

While the Japanese tended to ignore these phenomena in the 1960s, they became increasingly evident during the 1970s. Throughout the decade of the 1980s, many of the misguided policies of sales and investments will come to roost and Japan's economy will suffer very seriously from the "doughnuts" and "boomerangs."

4
Long-Suffering Labor

Lifetime Employment For An Elite

So much has been made of "lifetime employment" in Japan, seen as the cornerstone of the management system, that many foreigners assume this phenomenon pervades the labor force. They are therefore amazed to learn that there is some turnover, workers are dismissed and yet others quit. How can this happen?

The primary reason is quite simple. "Lifetime employment" does not apply to all workers by any means. It only applies to a minority of workers who are in a particularly fortunate position, so much so that they are often referred to as the "labor aristocracy."

It is impossible to count the number of workers coming under lifetime employment because there is no such clause in labor contracts. Rather, this has become a custom and continues largely because it is tacitly accepted by both management and labor, albeit for different reasons. Thus, if either side feels the arrangement is not in its interest, it would tend to breach or just ignore the convention.

To get even a rough estimate of how many are covered by lifetime employment is not easy. It has been attempted by various specialists in labor matters and can probably be approached from two directions. The first is by subtraction, namely be seeing who does not usually benefit from lifetime employment.

Among those who would not are workers in most of the small and medium-sized enterprises in manufacturing and even more so in services or distribution trades. The stronghold of lifetime employment is among the larger companies, those with over 300 employees, which do not even represent 1% of all companies although they employ about 30% of the labor force. However, some of the smaller companies would also have it. Let's say about half of the workers are in such companies.

However, even in such companies, the work force consists of two basic components, "regular" employees and the others, either temporary, part-time or subcontracted. It is hard to tell just how many of them there are but about 20% would be a safe guess.

Moreover, women as a whole do not enjoy the fruits of lifetime employment. Most of them join a company shortly after graduating from school and are expected to stay with it three or four years before "retiring." If they do not retire gracefully, they may be encouraged to leave. Most do. Many women return to work after having raised their children. But those entering a company at such a late date never benefit from the system.

Subtracting workers in small and medium companies without the size or wherewithal for lifetime employment, then the non-regular employees in those companies where the system supposedly prevails, and then women on the whole, one gets a residual. It is perhaps a quarter of the labor force, give or take a bit. And that is all that really enjoys lifetime employment at best.

Working in another direction, we can take the number of unionized workers. After all, lifetime employment—no matter what its proponents may claim—is not a gift flowing freely from management. Historically, it was created by the struggle of the unions to obtain job security just after the war, namely at a time when losing a job meant losing one's livelihood. Since then, it has been enforced by the unions, by reacting to any attempt at dismissal of their members in good standing.

Thus, one reads of cases in which such dismissals have been prevented or rescinded through action of the unions or by bringing the case before the courts. For example, it turned out not to be possible to dismiss a worker who was late repeatedly, who feel asleep on the job, or who caused minor damages. In general, only grave misconduct can lead to dismissal.

At present, the unions represent only one third of the labor force, leaving the other two-thirds with no effective protection against dismissal. Again, these unions are concentrated in big companies, making the situation in smaller ones more fluid. More important, unions are strongest in the public sector, where lifetime employment for bureaucrats is nothing special. In the private sector, they are less prevalent and weaker. So, it would seem on this basis as well that only a quarter of the (non-civil service) workers benefit from lifetime employment.

As we can see, only a minority of the workers is covered by lifetime employment, the elite or aristocracy of workers. And this means that the others are much worse off. They serve as a buffer so that, in bad times, they can be laid off or forced out with relative ease making it possible to carry the lucky ones through more years of lifetime employment. Since they are the buffer and regular employees are not fired, the ordinary worker is exposed to even greater chances of losing a job than otherwise.

Thus, it turns out that there are very considerable levels of turnover in certain categories. Workers in small factories, especially subcontractors, have no tenure to speak of. Employees of construction firms are often hired, and fired, as each job is begun or completed. Workers in restaurants, hotels, or retail shops are not much better off. And women in general rarely hold any job longer than five years.

This relative weakness of lifetime employment may come as a surprise to outside observers. It was built up so much by foreign experts and Japanese managers that it was assumed to exist in the purest form. Yet, almost as soon as it was praised by the first foreigner to "discover" it, it was denied by Japanese experts who unfortunately wrote largely in Japanese and thus were not read abroad. Nor does one ever bother asking, or listening to, Japanese workers, who might have a very different view from their bosses.

Another interesting point is that, although this is seen as a manifestation of traditional attitudes of protection by the patron and loyalty of the beneficiary, the system is anything but ancient. In fact, lifetime employment as it is known today did not exist in the early period of industrialization, nor did it exist before the war. During that whole period Japan had rather high rates of turnover just like other industrial countries.

Only after the war was it institutionalized. The reasons were that the workers needed security *and* management needed a constantly growing work force at a time of rapid expansion. Now, the workers still want security, but management is not happy. During a recession, when expansion ceases and retrenchment is necessary, the company wants to be able to dismiss excess staff.

So, even while foreigners admire the system, there is much controversy over it in Japan. Although views may differ on certain aspects, almost everyone agrees that there is a serious crisis in lifetime employment. Some think it will be altered drastically in the coming years, others that it may disappear. But no one expects it to remain the same.

Instilling Company Spirit

Over the past few years, the flood of articles about the Japanese management system has swollen to the point that scarcely any literate foreigner is unaware of its miraculous success. The key elements are described in very high moral terms. The company offers "lifetime employment," "concern for the workers," and an atmosphere of "harmony." This kindness, or so we are told, is reciprocated by the staff which shows "discipline" and "loyalty."

There is no doubt that the system has been effective thus far. But this is certainly not only because of these admirable virtues. Other, very different influences are also at work.

For example, why do so many employees stick to their company? Much of the credit must be given to seniority-based wages and promotion. Any employee who has spent as little as five years with one company knows that he will have to accept a substantial drop in wages if he goes to another. A worker with ten or fifteen years seniority would scarcely think of such a move. Moreover, the structure of companies is such that only smaller, more humble ones would even accept someone in mid-career. So it is both foolish to leave the present employer and extremely difficult to get another reasonable job elsewhere. That is more than enough cause to show loyalty.

The hard work stems from the small group system, also much praised. No one mentions that Japan has worked on the basis of small groups assuming joint responsibility in the nationalist and war period, in the earlier Meiji period, and the old feudal age. Small groups have many fine features. They permit the members to know one another, to develop a team spirit, and to work harmoniously together. But that is only part of the story. Small groups can also be controlled more readily by management, for they tend to keep their own members in line.

We all know that Japanese work very long hours, coming in before the official opening time and staying long after the closing time. That is a manifestation of "loyalty," if you will, but also of the social pressures at work. The young employees arrive early and leave late because their boss does the same, and to do anything else, in a highly conformist society, would mean to stand out as different and perhaps also unreliable. Whereas once those long hours could be justified by work, they now often become ludicrious in a recession when employees sometimes have nothing better to do than read newspapers, chat with colleagues, drink tea or play chess. Yet, they would not dream of leaving the office on time.

This also helps explain why so many foremen or middle managers still do not take the vacation granted them. Is it due to dedication to the company? Perhaps a bit. More likely it is because they know full well that any work that accumulates for them will be held over until they return or done by their colleagues. To avoid imposing a burden on fellow group members, they prefer not to take vacations. Since the bosses don't take vacations, many of the younger employees would not dare to either.

Unfortunately, this phenomenon can go yet further. In many Japanese factories, there are no relief workers, something inconceivable in a Western factory or indeed any well run factory. What does this mean? It means that if any worker is absent, because he is sick or even hospitalized, there is no one there to replace him. Instead, either the foreman takes his place or the other group members have to carry the burden. No Japanese would wish to impose such burdens on people he is close to.

It is such subtle pressures that keep the Japanese busily at work and so diligent they would not even take a day off. In a few cases, however, the manipulation goes so far that it becomes perfectly clear even to an outsider. One case involves menstrual leave for women. According to law, women who have a difficult menstruation can take a few days off. Yet, when someone asks for leave, the management often announces over the public address system that such-and-such a lady will not be showing up because. . . . Japanese women are very sensitive and readily embarrassed. Such treatment is enough to prevent all but the hardiest from taking their rights.

Perhaps some readers know about the extraordinary system many of the Japanese automobile manufacturers boast of, where each individual worker is able to stop the assembly line if he falls behind or makes a mistake. This supposedly gives him more freedom and control over the pace and quality of work than in the West. Alas, according to someone who worked there, that is only part of the system. When any worker does stop the assembly line, a red lamp lights up above his post so everyone will know who is in trouble. Then, everyone will have to put in overtime without pay to get the unfinished work done. In the tightly-knit groups of Japan, no member would like to be held responsible for making his buddies do extra work.

Then there is the famous suggestion box. The Japanese, they say, *voluntarily* contribute untold thousands of precious suggestions to management. This contribution, however, is less spontaneous than it might seem. In some companies, there is a quota, say five suggestions a month, which everyone must meet. If someone does not, pressure is brought to bear on his foreman, and he encourages the worker to contribute more. Elsewhere, there are charts displayed for all to see showing who has been making suggestions and who not. Once again, somewhat less subtle social pressure will get the desired results.

It is not as if the foremen, supervisors or middle managers were much better off than ordinary workers. They do enjoy more status, and have somewhat higher wages, but they are individually and collectively responsible for the behavior of those under them. They not only have to ensure that the actual work for which employees are paid is duly accomplished, they have to exercise moral leadership. They must therefore become "friends" and "advisors," giving of their own time and

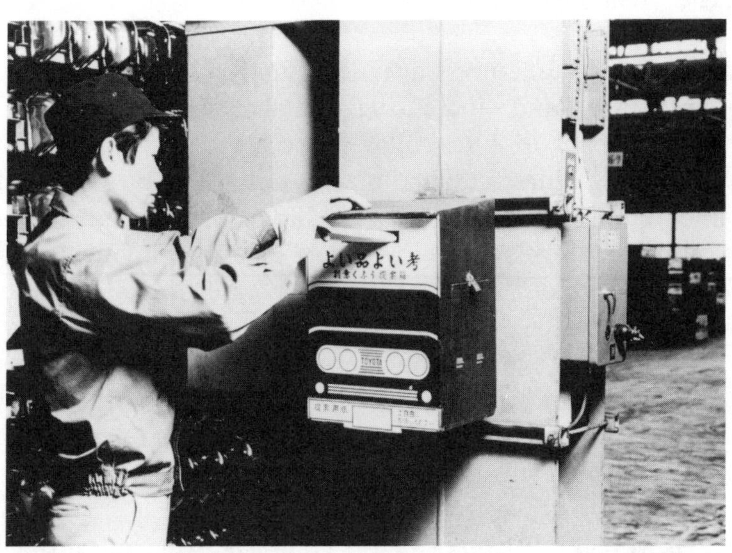

A suggestion a day keeps the supervisor away.

Credit: Toyota

money to socialize and even enquiring into personal and family matters that could affect the worker's morale. They must see to it that absences are few, that suggestions are many, and that no unpleasantness arises. But, to do so, they must exert any pressure gently if no less firmly so as not to impair the prevailing "harmony."

This should be more than enough to show that the typical virtues of the Japanese management system are hardly spontaneous. There may be some traditional basis and a feeling of mutual dependence. But management leaves little to chance in instilling company spirit, then reinforcing the institutional controls, and gradually harnessing the work force to its commercial needs. Under such conditions, it is hard to tell if these highly praised characteristics are virtues or vices.

The Disappearing Factory Hand

Japan's manufacturers are increasingly faced with a very unpleasant—and increasingly alarming—predicament: their supplies of blue-collar labor are drying up. From a country cursed with masses of unemployed and underemployed after the war, Japan has turned into a country with relatively low levels of unemployment and already a serious shortage in certain categories. How was this possible?

Part of the explanation everyone knows. Its industries expanded rapidly, absorbing labor from agriculture and the postwar unemployed. More recently, the tertiary sector has grown substantially and absorbed labor from the manufacturing sector.

However, this cannot be the complete explanation since Japan still has what for it is an exceptionally high level of unemployment, about 2.6%. This may not be very much when compared to the United States or Great Britain, but it is still about twice the general level of the 1960s and early 1970s. Yet, even with this mass of unemployed and other inadequately employed workers, not enough can be found to handle all the jobs in the factories.

According to the Labor Ministry, another 200,000 jobs have fallen vacant in the manufacturing sectors, bringing the total to about 800,000 skilled jobs which are looking for workers. And, no matter how many workers are also looking for jobs, there does not seem to be much chance the two will meet. For, the jobs do not suit the workers' requirements.

There was not much trouble about workers' requirements when Japan first began to industrialize because many of its manufacturers knew how to tap the existing labor supply. Their favorite source was not the industrial working class, namely children of other workers, but the farmers. The sturdy peasants, used to toiling long hours and adapting to the strict discipline of nature and the painstaking work of rice planting, did not complain about the conditions in factories . . . they were delighted to only work a regular eight hour day and know that they would be paid at the end of the week.

Farmers still provide much of the seasonal or temporary labor, accepting a stint in the factories during slack times. Others have become full-time workers, tending the farm in off hours or on weekends. But the number of farmers is rapidly shrinking. To catch what remained, many small manufacturers actually built their factories in rural villages to hire farmers on the spot. Now, even that solution is failing as the farm communities become depopulated.

The other ideal source was young women, once again more often from the countryside than the city, or perhaps lower class girls with little education. They would work a few years and earn enough money to set up house. However, nowadays young ladies do not like working in factories and much prefer the more genteel occupations of shop attendant or secretary. They can remain comfortable in air-conditioned stores and offices, look around for prospective husbands, and in the meanwhile not get terribly tired with their work.

The urban population has obviously also supplied workers, and increasingly the largest share of them. But this has been a rather choosy pool of labor. Young men and women with a college education traditionally enter white-collar occupations and hope to eventually become managers. Those who failed to get into college have to accept blue-collar jobs or other lesser occupations. This, by the way, will help explain why students are willing to undergo the horrors of examination hell since passing the college entrance exam is a crucial factor in deciding their future career.

In this vast category of urbanites, there has been a growing indisposition for blue-collar jobs. This results from a traditional contempt for lowly, unclean and unpleasant manual labor which is naturally combined with the modern snobbishness of preferring to work as a comfortable and secure salaryman in a big company. Things have only gotten worse as the younger generation developed its own preferences for leading a more independent and relaxed personal life and shirking the sort of discipline a factory job would imply.

But there is a second element which is peculiar to the Japanese labor market. Elsewhere, when a category of jobs becomes less attractive, that can be overcome by offering higher wages. This does not seem to occur in Japan. Many factory workers are bitterly annoyed by the fact that, after years on the job, they are still earning less than some young clerk or even than the salesman in a department store. A girl in a factory, toiling over an assembly line, would earn no more than another selling handbags in a classy boutique or running errands in a large trading company.

The reason for this is that the wage structure is not left to the whims of market forces but has been determined, almost once and for all, on the basis of society's value judgements. The primary factor in determining not only what sort of job one gets but also what one is paid is education. Pretty much by definition, a college graduate earns more than a high school graduate. Thus, employers which recruit high school graduates expect to pay less.

This is further strengthened by a second value judgement, namely the precedence given large companies over

Mixing business and pleasure. Calisthenics for the company.

Credit: Matsushita

small. Most of the workers are actually hired by small and medium-scale companies which do the mass of subcontracting work for the relatively few large ones which only engage in assembly (and this often highly automated). The smaller companies have a weaker position and have to accept the terms they get, which means they can offer their own workers less than the wage levels in the industry as a whole.

The outcome is that a blue-collar worker not only works harder, in worse conditions, than a white-collar worker, he also earns less. As a member of a smaller company, more often than not, he also enjoys less social benefits and the chances of being laid off are much greater. Is it any wonder that this sort of a proposition is increasingly rejected?

Of course, when young people decide that they don't really want to work in a factory, they do not usually go about trumpeting it in public. Such sentiments would still be regarded as improper in Japanese society. But, even while praising the nobility of manual labor, they get around the problem by doing everything they can to engage in more intellectual labor.

No student has to say that he doesn't want to become a factory worker. He simply strives to get into a college which automatically opens other perspectives. Thus, from year to year, the number of students continuing on to college has increased to the point where some 38% prefer further study to getting a job. This is well above the level of 24% only a decade ago and much higher than European levels if not quite up to America's 46%.

This is what creates the tremendous gap between supply and demand. What the factory owners want are high school graduates and about two jobs are offered for every one of them (at a time when there is only one job offered each college graduate and much less for labor in general). Not unexpectedly, nearly half the jobs go begging each year and companies complain of a labor shortage. Things are bound to get even worse as the workers they presently have continue aging and new ones are harder to find.

Naturally, they do everything they can to keep the factory going. Various expedients have been found to make up for the lack of young workers. One has been to hire more married women who return to work after their children grow up and who, in most cases, are doing so because they need the money. Older men who were laid off elsewhere are also recruited. But these sources are inadequate and hardly provide first-class labor.

Another possiblity has been to move the factory abroad to existing sources of plentiful and relatively cheap labor, like Korea, Taiwan and Southeast Asia. This migration has been going on for years and will continue. But obviously not all factories can make the trip. So, the last hope has been to increase automation and robotization. Yet, even here, smaller factories are at a disadvantage since they are usually doing the sort of work that is hardest to upgrade because it involves small parts, short series, or too much manual labor.

Thus, Japan's highly artificial yet implacable labor shortage will keep on growing and is bound to have far-reaching effects on the manufacturing sector.

Subcontracting Work And Worries

The Japanese employment system, in theory at least, is characterized by cooperative and harmonious relations between management and labor. This, of course, is a gross simplification because even here there is some friction and conflict between two groups with differing interests. But it is also a gross simplification for another reason that most outsiders ignore and most insiders keep secret.

This further breach in the highly touted Japanese system arises from the existence of a third and fourth group in the employment relationship. They are the management and labor of the subcontracting firms.

Subcontracting in Japan is not just an occasional or a secondary occurrence, it is an integral and fundamental part of the Japanese economy. According to the Small and Medium Enterprise Agency, itself a sub-body of the Ministry of International Trade and Industry, approximately 60% of the total number of small and medium enterprises are subcontractors. Such enterprises, by the way, account for about 99% of the total number of companies and 70% of the total labor force in the country.

This means that subcontracting is extremely widespread. While some of these firms depend entirely on subcontracting, others also have their own clients and some subcontract portions of their own work to lesser firms.

Whereas subcontracting is relatively limited in the service industries, it is truly pervasive in manufacturing and probably represents the bulk of both companies and workers in that sector. In some specific branches, such as machinery, motor vehicles, textiles and garments, shipbuilding, and construction, the amount of subcontracted work can amount to as much as 70%, 80% or even 90% of the total value of finished products.

Thus, the prime contractors and assemblers, those who turn out finished products and deal directly with the customers, have plenty of room to make use of subcontractors in order to get all the various parts and components they need or to accomplish assorted specialized or merely unwanted tasks.

But they can go much further. They can also exert

all sorts of pressure on the management of these weaker firms to make their own situation more comfortable. Most noticeable during the recession has been to squeeze the subcontractors for lower prices to keep their own costs down. In addition, it is not unusual to make the subcontractors wait 90 or 120 days for payment, or longer, to improve their own financial state.

Another approach has been to shift much of the burden for supply and inventory onto the subcontractors. The wonderful "just-in-time" system for which Japanese automobile assemblers are famous is not their achievement. All they really did was to force their subcontractors to manufacture, or deliver, when they were told to. It was the subcontractors who had to make the real effort to produce at the right time, to carry additional inventory if necessary, and then to deliver goods on the specified day and increasingly at the specified hour. They are not paid extra for that. Rather, if they do not comply, they would lose the work.

In addition, it might be added that most subcontractors never receive a written contract. They work on the basis of verbal commitments of the orderer, who can change them if he will. Nor do they enjoy much security in their status. If business is slack, their patron will simply stop placing orders and may even discard them and take in the work to keep his own staff and plant occupied.

In such ways, Japanese managers of large companies, those so highly praised abroad, solve their problems by passing them on to the subcontractors. They also enhance the position of their own employees by bearing down on the subcontractors.

Thus, subcontracting firms will be given the most painful, tedious and unproductive jobs while the more pleasant, mechanized and profitable ones are kept in-house. This means that much of the manual labor is carried out in subcontracting firms. And subcontractors actually send their own employees into the factories and shops of others to handle particularly onerous or dirty tasks.

Given the pressure of time, and the lower prices they can charge, the subcontractors' employees are usually forced to work much longer hours. They may have to give up weekends and vacations. Or, if work dries up, they may find themselves out on the street again. Very few enjoy such a thing as "lifetime" employment.

There is no compensation for this precarious and harsh situation in the form of higher wages. Quite to the contrary, according to all the statistics the employees of subcontracting firms earn less than those of the prime contractors or assemblers and they do not get much of a bonus or retirement benefits. The present gap in wages, for example, shows that those in small firms (5–29 employees) only earn 60% as much as those in large firms (500 employees or more). And the gap has been growing of late.

It is hard to imagine what life is really like for such workers since this is rarely seen by outsiders unless something exceptional happens. The recent coal mine disaster in Fukuoka, which led to subsequent investigations, offered one of these rare glimpess. For there, of 83 casualties, it turned out that nearly half were subcontracted laborers.

These employees worked in the pits with the other miners, but they did not enjoy the benefits of normal company staff and were not even members of the union. Many had worked seven days a week, and sometimes every day in the month, although that is formally prohibited by law. They were engaged in particularly nasty jobs, those regular workers did not want, such as cleaning ditches and carrying heavy loads. For this they were paid a meager ¥4,000 a day (with no bonus). And, even

The smaller the company, the lower the wage. Japan's "iron law."

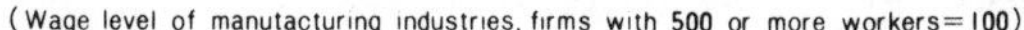
(Wage level of manutacturing industries, firms with 500 or more workers=100)

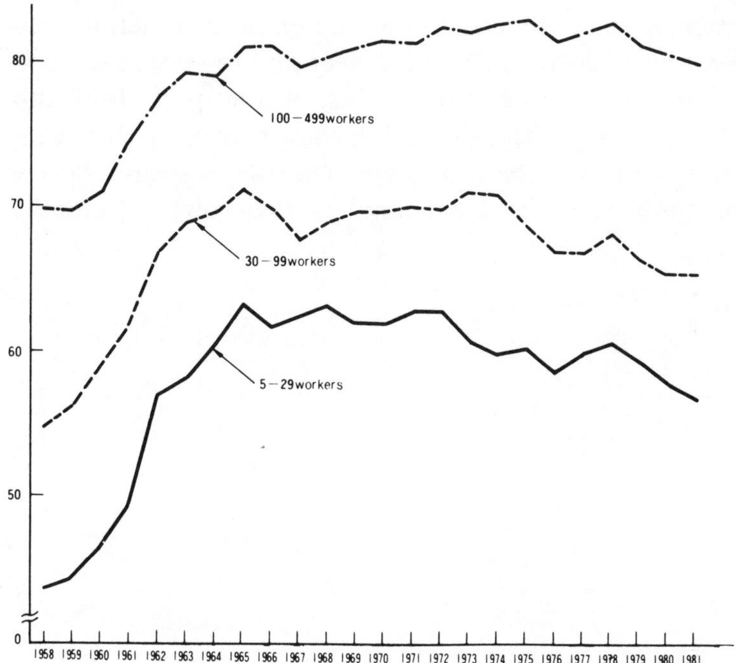

Source: *Monthly Labor Statistics Survey*, Ministry of Labor.
Credit: *White Paper on Small and Medium Enterprise 1983*, MITI, p. 31.

in death, they were discriminated against as their next-of-kin received much smaller consolation indemnities.

Another case which attracted the public attention a while back was that of the so-called "nuclear gypsies" who engaged in the dirty and dangerous work in nuclear power plants. They were the ones who also came into the greatest danger of radiation exposure. Yet, they were not employees of the rich and influential utilities companies but of tiny maintenance or cleaning firms. Even then, they were often hired by the day, paid a pittance, and periodically discarded.

While somewhat extreme, these examples are not atypical since the basic rationale of subcontracting is to keep costs down for management and to reserve the better jobs for company employees. Neither party finds this strange or reprehensible and, by subcontracting their worries to others, they manage to instill a greater degree of cooperation and harmony in their own relations.

5
End Of The Export Era

What If Protectionism Doesn't Go Away

When something goes wrong with the economy, the Japanese tend to take it very seriously and if that something is really bad they term it a "shock." There was a soybean shock in the early 1970s when President Nixon suddenly cut off American supplies of that essential foodstuff. Shortly after, there was the oil shock of 1973. And then came the second oil shock later in the decade.

Now the Japanese are reeling under an economic shock that is far worse than any other. But they are not talking about it. In fact, they try not to think about it or even admit that it has come about or could conceivably occur. This is the "export shock."

For a country working on the basis of import-process-export, an inability to sell goods is even more serious than an inability to purchase raw materials. Yet, as the years pass, the Japanese are finding it more difficult to place their exports. A look at the statistics will show that, although export value is still rising (part of this merely reflecting inflated prices), the rate of growth has slumped significantly. During the 1970s, which was not even that propitious a period, Japan's exports continued growing by an average 21% a year. This has since slipped to about half that level, with one year of distinctly negative growth (−8%) in 1982.

There are no valid economic reasons for this. Japan's products are not only as good as before, they are considerably better as regards quality and reliability. Price has not risen particularly, certainly not as compared to commodities or even competing goods from other countries. The yen weakened somewhat during this period, making Japanese goods even more affordable. And the Japanese commercial network is denser than ever, with offices of trading companies and manufacturers spanning the globe.

So, if the explanation is not quality, or price, or availability, there must be something else that is blocking Japan's exports. This can only be protectionism of one sort or another. And, perhaps fearing to admit it or thinking that an admission of its existence would only attract more protectionism, the Japanese have remained unexpectedly quiet and passive.

In this, they are abetted by their trading partners in Europe and America. As we all know, protectionism is a dirty word. It has therefore been replaced by more suitable expressions. There are things like orderly marketing, voluntary restraints, and lately a stress on reciprocity. But the result has always been the same . . . less exports.

Thus, at the present time, it is estimated that approximately two-thirds of Japan's exports are covered by one restriction or another. Textiles still come under various restrictive agreements. Steel is controlled by the trigger price mechanism and other means. Automobiles are bound by specific quotas, albeit voluntarily applied, in the United States and through other arrangements elsewhere. In Europe, depending on the country, there are limitations on ships, televisions, ball bearings, motorcycles, and so on.

But that is not the full extent to which Japan's export industries are hampered. Having finally realized that exporting their products too aggressively only resulted in nasty reactions, they are now moving more slowly even when there are no problems. To avoid any possible friction, doubtlessly at the behest of the government, makers of video tape recorders, machine tools, and other products are holding back somewhat even when they have orders.

What has this "export shock" done to the Japanese economy?

The stultifying impact can most readily be seen by looking at the progression of Japan's growth rates. During the 1960s, the economy was growing at a very impressive rate of over 10% a year. But that fell to a mere 5% or so during the 1970s. Part of this was evidently due to two oil shocks, but only part. Most authorities feel they only accounted for 2%, or at most 3%, of that drop. Some of the rest was certainly due to emerging trade frictions and conflicts. For the 1980s, largely as a result of mounting protectionism, only 3–4% growth is expected and it is not yet certain that can be attained.

Obviously, in the future, things could get better. If the United States achieves a strong *and* lasting recovery, if this impulse is dynamic enough to drag along the other industrialized nations, and if through some miracle the developing countries also participate in a general upswing, it would be possible for Japan to recover its old vigor. Yet, this increasingly looks like an unlikely scenario.

There is another scenario which, alas, is just as probable. That is that the world's economies will not really improve very much and, faced with growing trade deficits and unemployment, governments will be tempted to move toward more protectionism. This would naturally decrease world trade still further and hurt all economies. But, while all would be hurt, some would doubtlessly be hurt more than others.

Among the candidates for an economy which would be hurt most by protectionism, Japan is certainly very prominent. During more than three decades since the end of the war, it has grown rapidly thanks to relatively unhampered access to expanding world markets. Its economy, geared to producing exports and selling them massively, is now dependent on those markets. Any losses are immediately felt and are painful for the economy as a whole and certain branches in particular.

This is especially acute because Japan's exports, unlike those of many other countries, cover a rather narrow range of goods. Most of its exports are in specific categories of heavy industry or electronics, like steel, ships, automobiles, televisions, VTRs and now computers. In each of these industries, as much as half or more of total production is exported. And there are companies which depend on exports for as much as 80% and 90% of their turnover.

It is not hard to imagine how vulnerable this makes the Japanese economy. It was severely stunted by every blow to its exports and only recovered by coming up with new products that it could freely export. From textiles, to steel, to ships, to automobiles, to electronics. But, where can it go now? What new products exist which will be readily accepted in many markets? And, even if they are accepted, how much can be sold in a time of worldwide recession?

Thus, even if protectionism gets no worse, Japan's

economy is in for very rough sailing because it foolishly became over-dependent on exports. What would happen if protectionism got even worse is the sort of thing most Japanese do not think about or talk about, although they may feel in their bones that this is not impossible.

So, let us try a scenario showing just what this would mean and, this time, let us also consider the deeper implications.

To make things more realistic, rather than just inventing a theoretical possibility, we can consider one measure which was recently brought before the American Congress. Although it was rejected in that form, there is no doubt that new bills will be presented to impose local content legislation for the automobile industry. Under this, any company which exports more than a minimum number of cars, say 100,000, must have a specific local content which can rise as high as 90% for those selling more than 900,000 vehicles a year.

Whatever the figures ultimately are, the purpose is basically to force foreign makers to produce locally or keep their exports to rather minimal levels. In either case, the Japanese automobile industry would lose much of its export market. Considering that automobile exports to America presently represent about a quarter of total production, this would be a crushing blow.

But things will obviously not stop with this mere loss of American sales. As has happened in the past, when the American market is closed Japanese makers frantically try to make up for it on other markets, like the European ones. This results in surges and, somewhat later, measures to block exports to Europe. Taiwan and Korea with their own industries, other countries which assemble American or European cars, and so on might also want to limit Japanese imports. Only the Middle East and some developing countries would eventually remain open. This could decimate the other quarter of Japan's total automobile production that is exported.

To be magnanimous, rather than assume that the half of its production which presently is exported becomes blocked, let us merely assume that Japan loses a quarter of its total production. This is already enough to seriously handicap and perhaps cripple the whole industry. For, Japan's automobile plants (like everything else) are built for maximum economies of scale and this would be lost if they had to work 25% under their present capacity. In practice, the loss would not only hurt the makers domestically, by being less efficient they would find it harder to export even to those markets which remained open.

Of course, the loss of automobile sales by the Japanese would not be the end of it. This would mean that automobile manufacturers consumed considerably less steel, less rubber, less plastic, and less of the many automotive and electronics components that go into making cars. They, and the other related industries, would have to shed their excess workers and suddenly the economy would have to carry the burden of large numbers of unemployed.

This is what could be expected if the American Congress were to adopt strict local content legislation for automobiles. Perhaps this eventuality may not occur. But there are many others that are entirely possible and it is almost inconceivable that some of them will not be adopted to protect America's or Europe's ailing steel, shipbuilding, automobile, electronics and other industries. Protectionism is not only in the air, it is a patent reality that increasingly affects national policies.

As an export-oriented country, Japan would doubtlessly suffer more than others, including those whose recent problems seemed more serious. It is obvious that a continental power like the United States, or the Soviet Union and People's Republic of China for that matter, are better able to get by in a protectionistic world. They have their own sources of raw materials and a much bigger domestic market. European countries could also do better than Japan for, through the European Community and traditional trade links, they too have a much bigger market and close relations with Africa.

If protectionism were to spread, Japan would probably be hurt most. And that is why its leaders are so worried about the phenomenon that they prefer not even to mention it. While American, French and British leaders are still pleading against protectionism, the Japanese shun the word and praise an increasingly hypothetical free trade.

This may be a wise policy, since the more we talk about protectionism, the more we think about it, and perhaps the more it actually occurs. But making believe it does not exist is certainly not going to solve the problem.

Thus, it is highly regrettable that Japan has not done more to avoid the danger. This could take the form of energetic measures to open the Japanese market to its trading partners, measures whose value must be judged by actual increases in trade and not protestations of good will by the Japanese government. More could also be done to revamp the Japanese economy and boost the growth coming from domestic demand so as to make it less dependent on exports.

But the Japanese have done little of this. So, the export shock will be the most serious crisis they have to face. And they will find it more painful than anything in the past.

Export And Perish

There is no doubt about it, the Japanese know how to manufacture. They make first class products that are the envy of other industrialized nations. They also know how to sell, although it is usually a hard sell. They push their products, vaunting their merits and coming down on price if need be. The result is massive flows of exports to all parts of the world.

There is only one little thing they do not seem to know much about, namely how to turn a profit on what they export. They consistently ask less for their goods than could be obtained and often less than producers of goods that are not worth as much. Unfortunately, this is the most important thing. For the only rational purpose to manufacturing these goods can be to earn not only an acceptable return but as much as the market will bear.

That the Japanese are not charging as much for their exports as they easily could must be obvious. For, although there is a strong demand and Japanese products enjoy considerable popularity, they are not only not priced higher than local products but often much lower. In case after case, Japanese firms are angrily accused of predatory pricing and dumping. While such charges are hard to prove, there is no doubt that they would not even be raised if the prices for Japanese goods were closer to the going rate.

As for profits, most statistics show that the Japanese are not making much money out of their overseas subsidiaries despite the fact that they pay the same wages, utilities and raw material costs. Since they can borrow the high technologies of the head office and often import cheaper intermediate goods or finished articles, they should actually be earning much more than local competitors. But that does not seem to happen very often.

Just how well the mother companies are doing is harder to uncover, because Japanese companies are very reluctant to reveal their true earnings and are masters of creative accounting. But the general profit level in Japan is lower than in many parts of the world. In fact, to believe the National Tax Administration Agency, over half the Japanese companies are taking losses. While those which have become renowned for exports are rarely among them, they are clearly not making the huge profits one would expect such massive sales to generate.

That would not be at all surprising when one considers the Japanese approach to marketing. The basic policy is to charge as little as possible, use these low prices to increase market share, and with a little luck drive most other competitors to the wall. Then, when there are only a few makers left, it is easy enough to jack up the prices through collusion. Effective as this may be, such practices are not usually approved of in other countries.

Nevertheless, when the Japanese launch export drives, they also tend to charge less than they might. In the early days, this was because Japanese goods were not of very high quality and it was necessary to offer lower prices just to get in. Now those days are long past and Japanese quality is renowned. Their products are so good that they could readily charge more than their foreign competitors and get away with it.

But they don't dare to. They must think of their Japanese rivals who are also selling similar articles and carry the lust for market share and willingness to engage in cutthroat competition with them. Thus, even overseas, they countinually fall into the same sort of bitter struggles that are tolerated at home but repeatedly land them in trouble abroad. If they go too far, they will indeed be guilty of predatory pricing and dumping.

Thus, it must be evident that the commercial practices used by the Japanese are certainly not directed primarily toward financial reward and their businessmen are most definitely not driven by profit-maximization. As a matter of fact, a manager who increases market share while reducing profit would systematically be preferred to one who makes more money out of fewer sales. This is more than enough to explain the rather mediocre financial results of Japanese subsidiaries abroad and the not much better performance of their mother companies at home.

While exporting can be regarded as a corporate activity, it is also a national endeavor for the Japanese who work on the basis of import-process-export. So, it is extremely interesting to see how Japan succeds as a nation. This can be done by considering the terms of trade which balance increases in the unit price of exports

Export mania: from the factory, to the wharf, to foreign markets.

Credit: Toyota

against those for imports. While this is not flawless, it is a particularly good yardstick for an island nation like Japan where many of the imports are subsequently integrated in exports.

Simple as it is, this sort of calculation is not often done by the authorities and the terms of trade are almost never cited in public. That is comprehensible. Japan's terms of trade situation is almost disastrous. In fact, the level in 1981 was only 57 when taking 1970 as the base year with an index of 100. It has only improved slightly since. To show how poorly Japan is doing, it might be mentioned that the level of a place like Korea, in much the same sort of trading position, is at least 70. And it is far less admirable when compared to the advanced countries as a whole, which had a level of 79.

In its simplest expression, a level of 57 signifies that Japan's import prices have been rising nearly twice as fast as its export prices. That makes some sense since it was hit by two oil shocks and mounting prices for other raw materials. But that is only one side of the picture. The Japanese have also been extremely reluctant to raise their own prices. On the whole, they have accepted most of the burden of this unparalleled degradation of the terms of trade rather than passing it on to their customers like any sensible country. Thus the pitiful result.

It might be noted that 57 is not only a rather poor performance for terms of trade in some abstract manner. It actually involves a substantial shift of wealth from the country to its suppliers, who charge more, and, in another way, to its customers, who are not forced to absorb the higher costs. It could even indicate that, far from becoming richer, the Japanese have virtually become poorer due to trade. For, it would be extremely difficult to rationalize production enough to make up for costlier inputs. This implies that the producers were not really earning anything on some exports and taking a loss on others.

Fantastic as it may seem, that sort of interpretation cannot be entirely ruled out. A company which did nothing but export would be ruined. However, Japanese producers also sell their goods locally. This enables them to recoup any losses due to exports by boosting prices on the domestic market, something that is much easier to do since there are relatively few producers and collusion is rife. In the end, it is the Japanese consumers who pay for the producers' amazing inability to raise prices and make profits.

These findings oblige one to look at this supposedly superlative exporting machine in a very different light. If Japan exports goods to earn money and enrich the nation, even the unprecedented aggressiveness and frenzy to sell could be understood, for the people benefit from it. But, if there is a good possibility that they are actually draining the country of wealth while companies only turn mediocre profits, then the whole exercise becomes slightly ridiculous. It only creates turmoil in the world economy, friction in trading relations, and vast movements of products from which the Japanese gain little . . . and sometimes nothing.

The Export Squeeze

With its trade surpluses increasing again, reaching an unprecedented level of ¥20 billion last year, Japan is in serious trouble with its trading partners. They will not stand for such lopsided relations and will be particularly irate if its exports continue rising.

This is not the first time that Japan has been accused

of exporting too much. And it will not be the last. But the accusation is exceptionally bitter now because Japan's exports, for the moment at least, are not a sign of strength but of weakness.

Take the 1983 trade surplus, for example. The $20 billion was not a result of a major boost in exports. As a matter of fact, exports only increased by some 6%, which is quite minimal. The surplus resulted much more from the sluggishness of imports, which decreased by 4%.

This phenomenon was even more pronounced for 1982, when there was actually a slowdown of exports. For the first time in a decade, Japan's exports actually shrank by some 8%. Yet, its imports slipped even more, giving it a $7 billion trade surplus.

Alas, it does not help much to explain that the surpluses arise more from dull imports than dynamic exports. Its trading partners don't really care what the source is and they will remain aggrieved until something is done about it.

Moreover, Japan's exports are always a cause of irritation among its principal partners in the West because most of the growth comes from industries that compete directly with theirs and gradually wear down the local companies. The leading exports are all products which compete head-on with European and American products: steel, automobiles and motorcycles, electronics and computers, machine tools and now robots.

Thus, there are constant complaints from distressed firms which are hurt by falling sales. They air charges of dumping, predatory pricing, aggressive sales techniques, import surges and the like. This always makes Japan look like the main danger to domestic prosperity.

Meanwhile, another group of countries is vigorously stepping up exports to the very same Western countries.

The most prominent of them are the "newly industrializing countries" or NICs, including Korea, Taiwan, Hong Kong and Singapore.

They have not boosted sales by small increments like Japan. To the contrary, they boast export growth rates that are much higher. During the 1970s, when Japan's exports only grew by 21% a year, theirs gained between 30% and 40%. When Japan's exports fell by 8% in 1982, theirs managed to hold on or even grow. When Japan's exports increased a mere 6% last year, theirs rose by some 10% to 20%.

This was extremely bad news for Japan. For, having modeled their economies on its own, they sold much the same range of articles but in somewhat lower price or quality categories. Since the total market had hardly expanded, they were basically eating into Japan's market share. In some cases, they were actually driving out its products.

This applies especially to sectors like textiles and garments, footwear, toys, simple electronics and household appliances. However, as their industries upgrade, they have begun to add crucial items like steel and automobiles and may even rival it for VTRs and computers. Quite simply, there is no article for which Japan does not have to worry about present or future competition from the NICs.

One would think that these more forceful exporters would also come under strong pressure from the West. To some extent, they do and some restrictions have been imposed. But they are nowhere near as annoying or feared as the Japanese.

First of all, Japan runs a much bigger economy and its exports account for almost 7% of the world's total. With considerably smaller economies, not even Korea or Taiwan represent as much as 1% of world trade and Hong Kong and Singapore are much smaller. The impact is thus considerably reduced and it is easier for them to slip through the cracks of protectionism.

Secondly, given the mounting complaints and pressure, Japan has no choice but to move gently in selling its goods. It cannot afford to create any more friciton or displeasure since that would immediately result in new restrictions. This makes it harder to react to offensives by the NICs which can thus raid some of its earlier markets.

Thirdly, and perhaps most important, the NICs are not competing as directly with domestic industries. They only enter sectors which have already been breached by Japan and where the less efficient producers have since been crushed. By the time they arrive, there is scarcely any local industry left to complain. In this sense, Japan conveniently clears the path for them.

That the NICs then proceed to eat into Japan's market share hardly upsets the local population. They are happy to have even cheaper consumer goods and to find that competition between suppliers keeps prices down and expands choice. If the NICs beat Japan in this competition, the consumers could not care less. In fact, they may feel that it served Japan right.

So, Japan is definitely caught in the middle. Even when it increases its exports moderately, it causes all sorts of aggravation with its trading partners. But if it loses some of its market share to the NICs, it can count on no sympathy from them. Worse, it does not dare to react aggressively and push its own products because then it will be accused of more trade abuses.

Unlike the past, when increasing exports at least brought growth and progress, exports only spell trouble at present. They actually mean double trouble, on one side with its long suffering trading partners and on the other with increasingly obstreperous newcomers.

Suffering From "Goatism"

Those following the local media's coverage of the trade conflicts may have been surprised by repeated use of a strange Anglicism which has crept into the Japanese language . . . "goatism." This word has nothing to do with goats as such but very much to do with the more symbolic concept of "scapegoat." "Goatism" in general means making a scapegoat of someone. But it is hardly ever used in the general sense. It almost always refers to cases in which the Japanese have allegedly been made scapegoats by the outside world.

This term is not very old. It only became truly popular in the last few years. Yet, by now, it is used so widely that one cannot understand the state of the Japanese mentality without considering it. To grasp the deeper significance of the "goatism" phenomenon, it is much better to start with some recent examples.

A few years ago, Japanese automobile exports began climbing rapidly, especially in the United States and Europe. The sharp influx of Japanese cars brought about reduced sales for domestic makers which were already in serious difficulty. With some 300,000 workers laid off, the American trade unions began a struggle to block Japanese imports and this ultimately resulted in imposition of voluntary restraint on Japan.

In this case, the Japanese automobile industry was the "scapegoat." It was being punished by Japan's trade partners for being too competent, too efficient, and too aggressive. That, in the interim, Japanese automobile production had risen to the top position and Toyota and

Nissan were the world's No. 1 and No. 3 automakers, making them rather unlikely "scapegoats," was completely forgotten.

Naturally, the automobile giants which had to accept temporary restrictions were not the only sacrificial lambs thrown to the wolves in the Western world. Before them, there were the textile, and the steel, and the television manufacturers. There were also the shipbuildders. All of them had to face discrimination and pay the price of their superiority.

Now the time has come for a sophisticated product like video tape recorders. This was shown most blatently by France's controversial action. By adopting complicated procedures and restricting entry to Poitiers, it was struggling to keep out Japan's latest hit in consumer electronics. That the VTRs were a tremendous drain on France's foreign exchange, that there was already a substantial trade deficit, that the VTRs were occasionally sold at dumping prices and that imports surged was rarely mentioned. In Japan, it looked like a case of sheer jealousy.

But "goatism" has not only occurred when its trading partners tried to block Japanese products. It also arose when they insisted that the Japanese market be opened wider so that they could sell more goods. When it became impossible to obtain a broad opening or general measures, America or the European Community usually attacked a particularly noticeable product or company.

Thus, the first major "scapegoat" was NTT. This happened to be the nation's telephone and telecommunications monopoly, one of its largest companies, and one that was making very handsome profits. It was also a company which steadfastly refused to buy foreign goods and whose president at the time claimed that all he could use from abroad were "mops and buckets." So, it should hardly have been hurt by accepting foreign products, although this doubtlessly annoyed the local suppliers which previously enjoyed a protected market.

Another "scapegoat" was the tobacco monopoly. Through tariffs, quotas and restrictions on domestic advertising and marketing, it had managed to keep the foreign share of the market to a mere 1% for years. It fought like a lion (and not a lamb) to prevent their access once this was pressed by the Americans. Finally, under government pressure, it was forced to give in somewhat.

Of course, the saddest "scapegoats" at present are Japan's farmers. Heavily subsidized, protected by tariffs and quotas as well as a rigging of the market, and almost guaranteed a decent living come what may, they have increasingly complained that the nation's industrialists are trying to avoid America's wrath by turning attention to farm imports. Even the government, or so they insist, is willing to sacrifice them to restore peace with its partners.

But the most extraordinary case so far has been the IBM affair in which personnel of Hitachi and Mitsubishi were accused of illegally obtaining secret information. Although the facts were clear enough, over a period of months these huge electronics firms were turned from the perpetrators of a conceivable crime into the victims of IBM's machinations. In Japan, most of the reporting stressed the concept of "entrapment" as if this were just a vicious plot by IBM (and the American government, through the FBI) to humble and embarrass overly successful and basically innocent competitors.

These various examples of "goatism," and the stories woven around them in the media, present some common elements. Naturally, the Japanese are always the victims. That the companies involved are large, profitable and aggressive is unimportant and apparently does not detract from the idea that they are really being taken advantage of. It seems quite easy for the Japanese to endorse the idea that, in fact, they *always* end up the victims when dealing with foreigners, and especially Westerners. It even occurs that certain authors trace the origins of "goatism" back to the talk of a yellow peril and refusal of Japanese immigration many decades ago.

Not only are the Japanese victims, they are being punished for doing something intrinsically good. In the Japanese mentality, enhancing quality, improving efficiency and productivity, and exporting better products at lower prices is always conceived of as helping the rest of the world. This is Japan's contribution to international prosperity and well-being. That the goods are produced to make money or might compete with other goods abroad is rarely considered.

Thus, when the French government introduced its measures to restrict video tape recorders, one of the Japanese manufacturers responded with a full-page ad in *Le Monde*. It explained the case as seen by many Japanese. "We are not Saracens, we do not come as invaders to sow desolation . . . We offer our knowhow, better quality of life, greater reliability, and the beauty of sound and image." What could be wrong with that?

While accentuating the positive, the Japanese carefully avoid the negative. They do not like to talk about the fact that when exports increase too rapidly, and create trade surges, they hurt the partner's economy. The fact that there are already massive trade deficits suffered by many of these partners is ignored. If it has to be conceded that bankruptcies occur in the very same industries which receive the most exports, they see no correlation. And unemployment in those sectors is surely not a side effect of Japanese export drives.

If anything, these negative aspects tie up with—and are the counterpart of—Japan's success. The reason that other countries so readily accept Japanese imports is that Japanese products are superior. The reason they cannot export to Japan is that their own products are not good enough. They have low efficiency, inadequate machinery, and a bloated social structure which drains finance from productive purposes and spoils the population with welfare frills. Western productivity is also low because the people are increasingly lazy, they refuse to show up at work on time and then go off on strikes.

"Goatism" therefore has a second function, this time considerably less defensive. It permits the Japanese to compare themselves with others and, in a typically Japanese manner, to draw the conclusion that they are indeed better. Since they are trained to be modest, rather than build up Japan, they find it easier to tear down the others. Since any excessive glee at Japan's successes would anger its partners, it is safer to criticize what they must admit are weaknesses.

While "goatism" in both the negative and positive sense satisfies very deep emotional needs of the Japanese people, it certainly does not contribute to solving any of the world's trade problems.

First of all, by seeing themselves as "scapegoats" in so many unfortunate encounters with their trading partners, the Japanese are creating a laager mentality. They come to feel that little fairness can be expected of others and thus they should fight for as much they can get. When the others react, they must accept what is imposed on them. Such an attitude, while understandable in a truly weak country, is patently absurd for the world's third largest economy.

Secondly, by stressing the positive aspects of their trade offensives and stubbornly disregarding the unfortunate consequences they can have for others, the Japanese fail to take a balanced approach to specific problems. In many cases, it would not be necessary to restrict Japanese trade at all if they would understand the situation abroad and proceed more gently. However, if they refuse to concede that surges or excessive trade imbalances are of their making, then they cannot help to undo them.

Thirdly, by regarding themselves as the underdogs and those suffering from discrimination, it is very hard for the Japanese to show much compassion. Moreover, as long as it can be argued that most (if not all) of the failures of the trading partners are their own fault, there is little reason for the Japanese to make any concessions out of kindness or generosity and whatever is obtained must be gained by force.

More generally, however, it is unfortunate when normal problems between countries, be they economic, social or political, take on an emotional and nationalistic hue. "Goatism" is clearly an irrational explanation of what is happening and clinging to such an explanation is inherently unhealthy. It would be much better for Japan, and the world as a whole, if greater efforts were made to approach any conflicts rationally. Only then would there be much chance of finding mutually acceptable and beneficial solutions.

6
Running Out Of Money

Japan As No. 1—Public Debt

Japan has been busily catching up with the advanced countries in many activities. But no one thought it would seek to outdo its rivals in the race to fiscal irresponsibility and national insolvency. Yet, that is what it has been doing at an unparalleled rate.

Back in 1975, the Japanese government had no debts to speak of. Or at least none that caused much of a stir. For it did issue so-called construction bonds to cover the cost of roads, highways, bridges and the like that it could not pay for out of normal revenue. While small then, these bonds have been mounting at an extremely rapid pace since its revenues did not increase as quickly as the construction needs.

However, in that year, breaking one of its many pledges, the government began floating deficit-covering bonds. These were bonds issued to cover normal expenditures which, until then, had been paid for out of tax revenue and should always be funded by such sources in any well-run state. These bonds have been increasing even more rapidly.

Between the two of them, the amount of bonds skyrocketed and dependence on bonds as an easy way out became almost addictive. The level of deficit financing was truly monstrous. From 11% in 1974, it rose to nearly 35% in 1979, and then dipped somewhat. These levels were easily twice as high as in the United States, Great Britain, Germany or France. Worse, while the latter tended to reduce such dependence, Japan became hooked.

At the present time, the total amount of government bonds has swollen to ¥120 trillion. This breaks down to about ¥1 million per person and is already approaching the American and European levels, although they have a much worse reputation for profligacy than Japan.

What is more serious, however, is that while the situation is improving somewhat elsewhere, there is little hope that Japan will shake the habit. The government has repeatedly expressed its firm resolve to cease issuing new bonds and then buy back the old ones. The date originally set for the end of bond flotation was 1984. It has since been postponed to 1990. But no one expects that deadline to be met either.

The reasons are quite simple. This would require either a massive boost in taxation to increase revenue or a huge decrease in expenditures to save money. Neither of these is politically palatable and, at most, small steps will be taken in both directions so that the national debt will grow somewhat less swiftly.

But even this more optimistic scenario is being gravely undermined by the introduction of yet another type of bonds. Ten years after issuing the first deficit-covering bonds, they must be reimbursed and the amount of bonds that have to be redeemed each year will increase very rapidly (in keeping with the earlier expansion). Thus, a new—and inevitable—batch of refinancing bonds will soon appear although the government had insisted it would never go so far.

With all three forms of bonds growing at a jolly rate,

Japan as No. 1 for dependence on public bonds. Worse than the West.

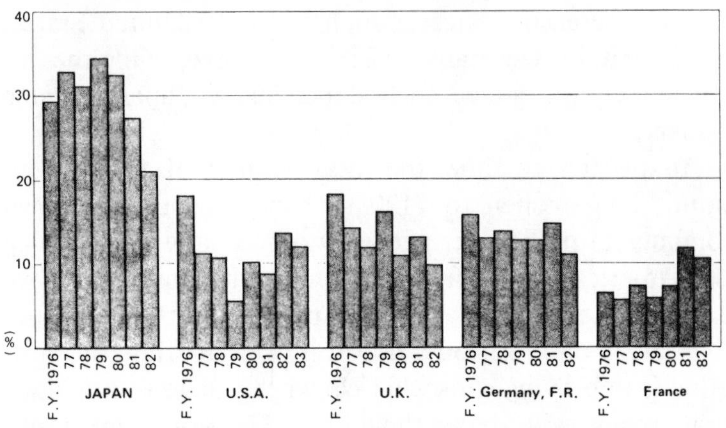

Credit: *'82 Japan*, Prime Minister's Office, p. 63.

Japan should be able to increase its ballooning debt to ¥200 trillion by the end of the decade and maybe ¥300 or ¥400 trillion by the end of the century. This would put it among the biggest debtors in the world, only slightly less notable than the Latin Americans because most of this money is owed to the people.

However, is this the total debt?

While the government does not talk about it, there are a few other items that should normally be included. The first is municipal debt, since the towns and cities have also been living beyond their means. Some of the shortfall was covered by the national budget. But the rest has had to be met by floating municipal bonds to cover about 10% to 15% of their annual budgets. These bonds already amount to some ¥45 trillion. With ever less money coming from the central government, these bonds may increase most rapidly.

There is a further item which is even more obscure. The government also runs what is known as the Investment and Loan Program for which it does not have to account to anybody. Many things that cannot be covered by normal revenue are paid out of this so-called "second budget" which is quite substantial, about two-fifths as big as the regular budget.

The funds come from the nation's postal savings system and pension schemes and should theoretically be invested in the most secure and remunerative manner. Instead, they are turned into loans to numerous government banks, public corporations and special agencies, some of them solid and reputable, others considerably more dubious.

Among the better uses is to finance the Export-Import Bank, Japan Development Bank, Overseas Economic Cooperation Fund and Housing Loan Corporation. But a lot of the money is spent on construction projects like the Honshu-Shikoku bridge or the new Osaka airport. Or it is entrusted in bodies like the Japan National Railways, Japan Railway Construction Corporation and Japan Highway Corporation. The chances of reimbursement here are much slimmer which means that, if they default, it is the central government which will ultimately have to pay.

This is not quite the end. The government also guarantees bonds which are issued by certain public or special corporations like Japan Air Lines, Nippon Telegraph & Telephone, Electric Power Development Company, Housing Loan Corporation and Japan National Railways. Given the growing insolvency of the latter, this could also be regarded as a form of government debt.

Taking one thing and another, it would be rather safe to assume that the actual government debt is roughly twice as large as the official figures that are usually cited. Instead of ¥120 trillion as a total and ¥1 million per capita, one could just as well speak of ¥240 trillion in all and ¥2 million per person. That is, for the moment. It will be much higher in a few years. Indeed, when it comes to public debt as well, Japan may end up as No. 1.

Fleeing The Fiscal Crisis

It was one of those curious debates that periodically enliven the Japanese political scene. It occurred in September 1982. The Ministry of Finance was becoming increasingly nervous about another major tax revenue shortfall. Its elite bureaucrats also noted that public debt was rapidly approaching the unheard of level of ¥90 trillion and, for the first time, debt servicing payments would reach nearly ¥8 trillion or about as much as the nation's social security expenses for the year.

Finance Minister Michio Watanabe, more blunt than his predecessors, warned that things were getting steadily worse and "it will be necessary sooner or later to proclaim something like a state of fiscal emergency." Prime Minister Suzuki topped this by announcing that the government's finances are "on the brink of bankruptcy." Former Prime Ministers Miki and Fukuda demanded that Suzuki promptly convene an extraordinary Diet session and declare a "fiscal crisis."

Then nothing happened. The newspapers were full of articles on the "fiscal crisis." Foreign media picked up the story and amplified it, making outsiders privy to the whole mess and unnerving those who had invested in Japan. So, instead of tackling the manifest crisis, the government and bureaucrats set about doing what they regarded as most important, restoring domestic and international confidence by denying that anything was wrong with Japan's finances.

This is what the English refer to as a "tempest in a teapot." But not quite. For there was a very serious financial crisis in the making and denying it, or making believe it did not exist, was no way of mending it. Rather, as we have seen, it merely permitted the situation to get progressively worse with total bonds exceeding ¥120 trillion and bond servicing passing ¥9 trillion not long ago.

The crisis assumes many forms and has many serious implications, only some of which can be dealt with here.

For one, and most obviously, as long as the budget cannot be augmented, it will not be possible to provide many things that the population wants or needs. It has become difficult to launch new public works and much of what is being done is merely maintenance of old projects. It is out of the question to hire enough teachers to make classes smaller. It is becoming impossible to provide adequate health care and old age facilities. Worse, the government may not be able to provide the social security people are entitled to.

In addition to domestic crimping, it will be too costly for Japan to fulfill many of its international commitments. Most notable is the pledge to boost the defense establishment, repeatedly made to the United States, and which its major ally regards as crucial. It is also proving impossible to expand economic cooperation as much as promised.

Limitations on the national budget have another dimension as well. Japan, more than most countries, has used increases in the budget, and especially in public works, to stimulate the economy when it is sluggish. With most items frozen, and public works actually shrinking in real terms, it is incredibly difficult for the government to pursue any active economic policy and the recent lackluster performance shows it.

Since even the present budgetary outlays would not be feasible without government bonds, it is necessary to consider the consequences of deficit financing.

One that is particularly worrisome, and already a nasty drain, is the need to pay ever larger sums merely to cover interest on the bonds, without yet redeeming any. Bond servicing is increasingly squeezing all other items in the budget although it is clearly the least fruitful for the nation.

The snowballing government bonds will take a heavier toll in the future. But it has already become an unpleasant burden for those who must purchase them, namely the banks. They would much prefer investing in more productive, and also more remunerative, operations. They only go along with this because they are pressured by the Ministry of Finance.

However, as more and more bank money gets tied up in government bonds, an onerous and long-term obligation, less remains for them to invest in companies. This will lead to a "crowding out" of the private sector which is the real lifeblood of the economy.

Of course, when anyone's debts rise too high, there is a justifiable fear of insolvency. As Prime Minister Suzuki pointed out during the "fiscal crisis," Japan's finances were on the brink of bankruptcy. Since nothing has been done to pull it back, it can only be assumed that the state is moving ever further in that direction. The only thing that has saved it so far is that its creditors are the Japanese citizens at large and they are relatively docile by nature and also not particularly eager to sink along with it.

The only solace they receive is government propaganda to the effect that Japan is really not so insolvent. Once again, it is not a question of being truly sound but simply that other countries are apparently even more overextended than it.

Looking at the statistics, it seems hard to bear that

out. Japan's level of deficit financing is among the highest in the world. Total debts are rising swiftly. They already represent nearly 40% of GNP, which is higher than any Western country. So, turning to another set of statistics, the government proudly announces that what counts is the ratio to net private savings. There, Japan does better than the United States or Great Britain, but not as well as Germany.

While that is comforting, it is hard to imagine what is meant. For the Japanese government cannot really rely on the people's hard-wrung savings to get it out of trouble. They are not going to buy bonds massively. Most assuredly not now, when an aging population is increas-

The strongest growth sector: printing government bonds.

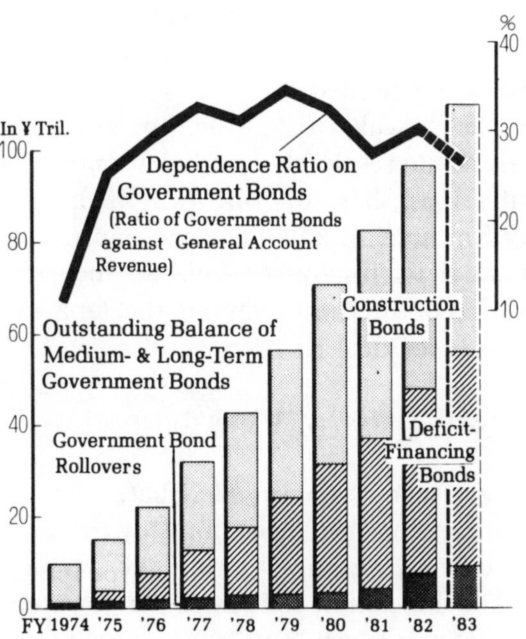

Credit: *Oriental Economist*, July 1983, P.5.

ingly in need of liquid cash. Unlike the banks, they cannot be coerced.

Still, in one way, the government is already dipping into the people's savings. This is through the trickery of the "second budget" which is fed by the postal savings and pension funds. One would normally expect such money to be carefully invested in gilt-edged securities and blue-chip stocks to appreciate as much as possible in order to pay good interest on the savings and provide comfortable pensions for the retired. Instead, it is used to buy government bonds and finance state banks that collect relatively low interest rates. Worse, some of it is channeled into public corporations, including the debt-ridden Japan National Railways.

This means that, without their knowing it, a big chunk of private savings has been converted into a sort of loan to the government. However, since that was not done fairly, there could be hell to pay if the money were not available when needed.

Thus, the "fiscal crisis" which the government decided not to tackle resolutely and has been hiding as much as possible since, has not gone away. It has stayed. And it has grown increasingly menacing and intractable with time. Until it is finally recognized, and suitably dealt with, it will continue undermining the Japanese economy and Japan's position in the world.

Paying Their Debts ... With Interest!

Every year, there is a heated debate over the budget. Politicians and businessmen staunchly demand that costs be kept down so as not to ruin the people and companies. The opposition condemns the government for increasing defense expenditures by as much as 6% or 7%.

There is concern lest social security or educational expenses get out of hand.

In this atmosphere, a consensus was reached on only allowing small increments in the budget and, lately, of holding most of it to a "zero increase." Very few exceptions are allowed aside from defense and, only partially, economic cooperation. And even then there are complaints of overspending.

Yet, there is one item in budget that is completely overlooked. It has not been subject to any debate, no committee was established to see how to reduce it, and yet it has shown the most vigorous growth of all. This item expanded by some 39% a year from 1973 to 1980, before the attempts at fiscal austerity. Even with the present stringent controls, it is still growing by over 10% a year.

This item is bond servicing. The government *must* pay interest on the bonds that were issued to cover the earlier budget deficits and, since the amount of bonds has increased, so has the cost of servicing them.

The progression was almost blinding. In 1973, only ¥443 billion had to be reserved for that task. By 1980, the sum had swollen to ¥4,344 billion, almost ten-fold. For 1984, the amount set aside is some ¥9,155 billion. And this is bound to continue with figures rising by over a trillion yen a year.

Moreover, back in 1973, the cost of bond servicing only represented a mere 0.03% of the total budget. By 1980, it had climbed to 10%. In 1984, it accounts for 18%. No one knows where this will end.

During this past decade, the amount of revenue being devoted to bond servicing has snowballed to such an extent that this item is almost the biggest one in the whole budget. The only category that is still larger is social

Ministry of Finance officials apportioning funds to other ministries.

Credot: Foreign Press Center/Kyodo

security. But more money is spent on servicing this debt than is provided for economic cooperation, or defense, or education and science. As a matter of fact, for 1984, bond servicing costs as much as the three of them put together.

It is therefore mind-boggling that so little attention has been paid to this single item that is absorbing more and more of the limited public funds and cannot be stopped like other expenditures. Moreover, while the continued flotation of bonds can still be regarded as a medium-term problem with some time left to find a solution, interest has to be paid on the old bonds now. This is the cutting edge of the fiscal crisis.

The only valid solution to both problems, ballooning national debts and bond servicing, is to increase taxes. But the Japanese, so financially responsible and conservative in their private lives, have taken the seemingly easy way out in public affairs. Rather than pay today, they issue more bonds in order to pay tomorrow and accept the penalty of interest fees.

This, alas, is a very bad deal. The money the Japanese are saving, if put in the bank, would only yield 4% or 5%. The interest they have to pay on bonds is 7% or more. It is obviously better to pay today rather than tomorrow and save the differential.

Some Japanese, however, assume that if the repayment can be postponed long enough someone else will have to pick up the tab. Who else can that be than their children and perhaps grandchildren? It hardly seems fair that the generation which benefited from the expenditures should pass the costs on to coming generations and burden their own offspring. But that is what they are doing.

Stil!, so far there is no sign that the Japanese have become aware of the ramifications of the debt servicing problem. The deadline to cease issuing government bonds was put off from 1984 to 1990. This date does not look much more feasible to the Ministry of Finance. And bonds will probably be floated well into the next decade.

Moreover, ceasing new bond issues is not enough to absorb the old ones, so the total amount of bonds will remain very high until the end of the century or later. That is how long the Japanese will have to pay for this strange mixture of profligacy and avarice that leads them to live beyound their means year after year.

During much of this time, the problem will not become more manageable. To the contrary, it can be expected that the cost of bond servicing will grow as will its share of the total budget. It is not even excluded that one yen in three or even one yen in two of tax revenue will have to be earmarked for paying off past debts rather than engaging in new and increasingly necessary expenditures.

If the whole budget does not increase substantially, not only will bond servicing become by far the largest item, all the others will have to be reduced correspondingly. There will simply not be enough money left over for such petty things as education and science, international cooperation, public works or defense. And social security or welfare will have to be very skimpy.

Perhaps then the Japanese, both the government and the people, will open their eyes and take a closer look at a much neglected budgetary item that is rapidly becoming the biggest threat to their future prosperity and well-being.

7
The Policy Gap

Japan's Nonexistent Economic Policy

After three long, lean years of recession, the Japanese economy is finally stirring. Every few months, it had been promised. But it was not until the spring of 1984 that recovery was clearly on the way.

Given the extraordinary importance of economics to this island nation, it is worthwhile asking two crucial questions. Who was responsible for bringing about the recovery? And, how was it done?

Normally, one would assume that the answers should be very simple. The government is responsible for economic policy and, with the businessmen, should be able to take any necessary measures. Just which policy tools are used, when and how, would depend on their reading of the situation and ability to wield them.

Unfortunately, going through the whole dreary period very carefully, it looks as if neither the government nor the businessmen had much to do with stimulating the economy. Few measures were taken and most of them were half-measures at best. As for the tools, they were either forgotten or poorly used. In fact, it could almost be claimed that Japan had *no* economic policy during this trying time.

The first thing a Japanese government usually does

when the economy slows down is to revive it with injections of government spending. This is a form of pump-priming that was used very actively in the past. The basic mechanism is to boost budgetary spending in general, and public works in particular, so as to keep money circulating and get people back to work.

This reaction, almost habitual by now, was severely hampered by the growing fiscal crisis which made it impossible to expand the budget much. Although public works were initially sheltered, they were eventually limited to minimal and then zero growth which meant, in practice, that the actual amounts involved were lower due to inflation. Thus, if anything, this had a negative impact on the economy.

During much of the period, interest rates were uncommonly high which also had a stultifying effect on the economy since businessmen found it too expensive to invest in plant and equipment and potential home owners could not afford loans. It was readily conceded, and repeatedly urged, that the interest rates should be lowered. But they were not. For, if they were, more money would flow toward the United States where interest rates were much higher, and the yen would continue devaluing, thereby causing friction with Japan's trading partners.

Monetary expansion might have been one way of solving the problem. But, after a nasty bout of inflation, the authorities were seriously worried about the results. Indeed, with inflation seen as a greater threat than slow growth, there was not much thought of turning in this direction.

Fiscal policy, at least, was under the control of the Japanese government and no foreign country could complain about how that tool was utilized. Actually, the American experiment with Reaganomics was extremely well known and some Japanese argued that, by adopting a large-scale tax cut, the economy could be revived.

Yet, while the suggestion was made, and then considered, it took three years to reach a decision. The outcome was to offer a rather minor tax rebate which could hardly be expected to generate much spending. And even that was largely nullified by the introduction of several new indirect and corporate taxes. This made fiscal policy about as futile as pump-priming, interest rate manipulation and monetary policy.

This meant that the economy was pretty much left to its own devices. Under such conditions, it has usually been exports which pointed the way. But this was obstructed by two increasingly worrisome developments. Protectionism was spreading perceptibly and it was feared that any conspicuous offensives would only bring about more restrictions. So, exporters exercised more restraint and caution than otherwise. And even what exports were permitted were less fruitful than usual since purchasing power was weak abroad.

The only remaining source of growth was therefore domestic demand. If only the Japanese could get their own people to buy more. Yet, the attempts here were no more productive. The reason was quite simple. Income had been growing very slowly and much of the gains were eaten up by inflation and higher taxation. Not only was there hardly any more money to spend, Japanese families were increasingly worried about the future and saved more, spending less.

In these circumstances, it was not surprising that businessmen tended to invest less in plant and equipment. With sales stagnating, it did not make much sense to expand production. Only machinery and robots to rationalize operations fared well. But they contributed to unemployment which, for the first time in decades, became a noticeable problem.

The government was therefore limited pretty much to short-term and rather tacky expedients. Interest rates might be lowered slightly, after it was clear that this would not have much effect on exchange rates. There was a tax rebate of sorts, although most of it was bound to be returned to the government due to new taxes. There were some incentives for plant and equipment purchases and the number of home owners receiving state housing loans increased somewhat.

This left the periodic packages of "stimulatory" measures embarrassingly flimsy and unconvincing. In fact, the only thing that had much of an effect was the front-loading of public works. The bulk would be spent in the first few months, which did result in a spurt of activity. But business was duller than ever during the rest of the year once the money ran out.

Thus, the only reason the Japanese economy has finally started moving again is that it was pulled forward by an upsurge in the United States and later Europe. It was these supposedly weaker and debased economies which had the inner reserves to revive on their own and then began accepting more Japanese exports. This, in turn, sparked Japan's recovery.

Hit-And-Miss Planning

Far more than the socialist countries which originated it, France which applied it to a mixed economy, and the developing nations which put blind faith in it, Japan has been regarded as the most successful country in the world when it comes to planning.

One early admirer, Norman Macrae of the London *Economist*, claimed that the Japanese economy is "the most intelligently dirigiste system in the world." According to him, "the ultimate responsibility for industrial planning, for deciding in which new directions Japan's burgeoning industrial effort should go, and for fostering and protecting business as it moves in those directions, lies with the government."

Even now, despite the slowdown in the economy, most outside observers tend to lend credence to plans adopted by the Japanese government even when they scoff at those of others as being hopelessly optimistic or overambitious. Japan's planning ability has thus become one more of the myths that proliferate.

Yet, if one takes even a quick look at the actual plans issued over the past decades, it becomes impossible to maintain much respect for Japan as a planner.

The first thing to note is that Japan has launched no less than ten plans, programs or prospects during the period from 1955, when the first was adopted, to 1983, when the most recent was approved. The average life of each attempt was therefore something like three years although they were all designed to cover a time frame ranging from five to ten years.

This means that most of the plans had to be drastically revised, revamped or simply scrapped within about half the time they were intended to serve the nation as a fundamental and solid guide to conduct. With such constant change, it was almost unfair to refer to these documents as medium or long-term plans since they were hardly more than short-term guesstimates.

More serious is how well the plans, programs and prospects charted the future course of the economy, thereby showing that government policy was effective and that the private sector had followed through. A cursory glance at the results will show that, once again, contrary to expectations, they were not particularly accurate.

Most of these documents included forecasts of the

Planning is easy. Only the implementation is hard.

Name of Plan	Dates Initiator	Growth Target (Actual Growth)
Five Year Plan For Economic Self-Reliance	1956-1960 Hatoyama	5.0% (8.7%)
New Long-Term Economic Plan	1958-1962 Kishi	6.5% (9.9%)
National Income Doubling Plan	1961-1970 Ikeda	7.2% (10.7%)
Mid-Term Economic Plan	1964-1968 Sato	8.1% (10.6%)
Economic And Social Development Plan	1967-1971 Sato	8.2% (9.9%)
New Economic And Social Development Plan	1970-1975 Sato	10.6% (5.3%)
Economic And Social Basic Plan	1973-1977 Tanaka	9.4% (3.8%)
Economic Plan 1976-80	1976-1980 Miki	6.0% (5.0%)
New Seven-Year Economic And Social Plan	1979-1985 Ohira	5.7% (c. 4.0%)
Prospects And Guidelines For The 1980s	1983-1990 Nakasone	4.0% (-)

growth rates for gross national product, production in various sectors, income, expansion of trade and payments, incidence of inflation and so on. The most important item, the one every plan is known for, of course, is the GNP growth target. And, if that is poorly predicted, it can be assumed that most other indicators are mistaken as well.

The least that can be said about Japanese planning throughout the three decades is that the targets were not only frequently off, they were almost never achieved.

The discrepancies were not minor either. Actual growth has turned out to be nearly twice as much as predicted, or barely half as much, on several occasions.

Admittedly, there were two very distinct phases in this process of error. During the 1950s and 1960s, the planners were consistently low in their estimates. The economy proved more responsive and dynamic than expected and it was repeatedly possible to grow faster than foreseen by the plan.

Thus, in the very first plan for fiscal 1956–60, adopted by the Hatoyama administration, only 5.0% growth was forecast while as much as 8.7% was attained. The results were similar for the Kishi plan and also the famous national income doubling program of Ikeda when Japan's highest postwar growth of 10.7% was achieved for fiscal 1961–70.

However, under the Sato administration, things began to change as the economy slowed down. His first plan was still exceeded somewhat. But the second, for fiscal 1970–75, turned out to be much too ambitious. The target of 10.6%, the highest ever posited by Japan, was far above the reality of 5.3%.

Indeed, as of the early 1970s, the tendency switched completely from one to underestimate growth to one to overestimate it. Events never worked out as well as hoped. While many observers trace this to the oil crisis and its aftermath, that only explains the poor economic performance . . . not why the planners and government stubbornly predicted much better results.

For example, although the economy was already winding down, the economic and social plan adopted by the Tanaka administration remained extremely bullish. This can be explained by the nature of the prime minister in part. But the planners and economists, who should have known better, still went along with and actually encouraged his dreams of reshaping the Japanese archipelago and creating an affluent society based on a strong growth trajectory of 9.4% for fiscal 1973–77. This was not to be, due only partly to the oil crisis. The actual outcome was 3.8%.

But this was not quite enough of a lesson. Under Miki, a much more modest politician, economic growth for fiscal 1976–80 was forecast as 6.0%. It ended up being only 5.0%, a disappointment only to those who really believed the economy co· ld do better.

Even that was not enough. By the time Ohira adopted the economic and social plan for 1979–85, the oil crisis had struck, the economy was sluggish, and a worldwide recession was setting in. Yet, the planners ambiguously talked of aiming for "slightly less than 6%" growth.

This was only defined more precisely as 5.7% when the plan was adopted in August 1979. But it was lowered to 5.5% in August 1981. And then the plan was just scrapped since it was evident that the final result would be closer to 4%.

Indeed, at about that time, Prime Minister Nakasone had had enough of planning, which he regarded as a faintly socialist practice unworthy of Japan, and insisted that a looser document be drawn up. Known as the "prospects and guidelines for the 1980s," it was terribly vague when it came to hard predictions and included very few targets aside from 4% growth for the fiscal 1983–90 period. Yet, many other forecasters felt the country would do well with something closer to 3%.

This should be more than enough to prove that, when it comes to planning, the Japanese are not the masters they are presumed to be. In fact, planning doesn't really seem to be their forte at all.

Imposing An Unneeded Austerity

Anyone who has followed the Japanese scene recently cannot fail to have noticed that the country's economic policy is not really determined by Prime Minister Nakasone or the bureaucrats in the Ministry of Finance, MITI or Economic Planning Agency. Rather, the primary responsibility for this has been assumed by three old men in their seventies and eighties who are in charge of the leading businessmen's associations. Anywhere else in the world, they would be regarded as fading relics of the past. In Japan, they are calling the shots.

The most prominent at present is Toshiwo Doko, who is the former president and still honorary president of the Federation of Economic Organizations (Keidanren), which groups the largest and most influential companies. For two years, he chaired the advisory Ad Hoc Commission on Administrative Reform, which drafted a number of reports and recommendations, and has since become the chairman of the supervisory Administrative Reform Promotion Council which is supposed to implement them.

Backing him strongly is the present president of Keidanren, Yoshihiro Inayama. He shapes the policy of big business and has to impose it—with considerable success of late—on the politicians and bureaucrats. Like Doko, he shows a considerable nostalgia for the past. However, whereas Doko merely lives in a state of frugality despite his wealth, Inayama has taken to preaching a return to the good old virtues of yore. His policy has been summed up as one of "bear and endure." If the Japanese would only pull in their belts, devote themselves diligently to work and forget about more wordly pleasures, they would be better off.

The third is Bunpei Otsuki, president of the Federation of Employers' Associations (Nikkeiren). This consists of a very broad range of companies and backs them in their labor-management relations. Its primary task is to handle the annual wage negotiations or *shunto*. Otsuki is now vice-chairman of the Administrative Reform Promotion Council. But he is even more noticeable for his insistence that the workers accept ever smaller wage hikes, even toying with the idea of giving them no increase at all.

What clearly unites these three old men is the preference for a policy of austerity as the answer to Japan's present economic difficulties. Most of them, they seem to indicate, could be overcome by pushing through an administrative reform, avoiding tax increases, and keeping wages as low as possible. In addition, they would like a return to the old virtues and old attitudes with more respect for traditional ways of doing things and a stronger work ethic.

The cornerstone of their program is very evidently the administrative reform. Various proposals have been made to reduce the activities of certain ministries, to cut down on the number of personnel and to return some state corporations to private ownership, especially the deficit-ridden Japanese National Railways. They also want to merge some of the lesser agencies and get local governments to pull back as well. This would leave Japan with a small and lean bureaucratic apparatus.

While not particularly stressed, the main purpose of this exercise is to avoid an otherwise inevitable rise in taxes which it is feared would hit the companies hardest. Although it is not really part of the official policy, the three old men and their organizations lobbied hard against any tax reform. They were not in favor of the value added tax that was earlier proposed by the Finance Ministry, they remained adamantly opposed to any raising of corporate taxes, and they were not even happy about the minor fiscal levies on consumer goods that were adopted.

Naturally, with no increase in taxes and any savings from the administrative reform likely to accrue at a later date, it has been necessary to keep the national budget down. This resulted in a freeze of most budgetary headings over the past two years and an actual cut for some this year. One of the few items that were permitted to grow is defense. Those that have been cut back are primarily social welfare, health and education. Yet, to save money, this year even public works have been reduced by 5%.

Once again, while not part of the official policy, the mere fact of refusing additional taxes and the inability to reduce the budget yet more, has resulted in a tacit acceptance of deficit financing. It had originally been intended to cease floating deficit-covering national bonds

The old men who run Japan's business organizations: Sasaki, Otsuki, Inayama, and Nagano.

Credit: Foreign Press Center/Kyodo

by 1984. Now that is expected to take until the end of the decade. In the meanwhile, Japan will continue to have deficits that amount to as much as a quarter of the total budget.

Last, and certainly not least, they have done their best to keep down wage increases. Nikkeiren and the managers of individual companies have gradually imposed their will on the weak enterprise unions. The level of wage hikes has sunk from year to year. For 1983, the average wage increase was a mere 4.4%, the lowest since the postwar recovery began. While they were certainly pleased about that, they seem to have forgotten that this was bound to undermine consumer spending as well . . . which was certainly not a goal.

This then is the policy imposed by the old men and formally accepted by Prime Minister Nakasone and his predecessor Zenko Suzuki. To say that the policy is popular would be an exaggeration. While the average citizens are pleased that the bureaucrats are being forced to share the burden, and certainly do not want to pay more taxes, they are not happy about the freezing of health and social expenditures. They do not approve of the weakening of the meager welfare system that was being created and they certainly do not like the squeeze on wages.

The policy is obviously none too popular with the bureaucrats. They do not appreciate being made the butt of a national campaign which places most of the blame for inefficiency on them. They do not like the loss of status as the three old men assume prerogatives that were once held by the bureaucrats. On specific policies, like the need to raise taxes and avoid deficit financing, there are strong objections in the Ministry of Finance. And both MITI and EPA would prefer some stimulation by the government.

Even part of the business community is unhappy. These are the smaller companies which depend much more on domestic sources of business. The construction companies, in particular, live largely off government projects and public works. Now that they are blocked, their own earnings suffer. More generally, many business leaders also feel that what the country needs most is a stimulative policy that is completely impossible in the midst of the administrative reform campaign.

But they have not been able to turn the three old men from their self-appointed task. Nor have they been able to convince Prime Minister Nakasone that he should not make administrative reform his primary economic goal and let it incidentally determine most other economic policies. The reasons for this incredible power over the govenment, while rarely mentioned in public, are not hard to find. It is the business community that has always pulled the strings quietly and from a distance due to its financial contributions to the politicians and parties. Now that it has openly committed itself to a policy, its wishes cannot be disregarded.

Thus, Japan will continue following the policy of austerity for as many more years as the three old men manage to overrule their juniors and dominate the government and bureaucracy. Whether they will actually attain their aims is less certain. After all, the budget deficits are so large that no matter how hard they try they cannot really compress expenditures enough to avoid all tax hikes. Nor can they afford to let the government bonds accumulate because this would crowd out investments by the private sector. So, one day taxes must be increased.

Until then, however, this policy will be forcing the Japanese people to go without many things that are part-and-parcel of any modern society. Social security benefits will not be able to keep up with the needs of a rapidly aging population. Unemployment insurance, hardly existent today, cannot be expanded to help the growing number of jobless. The health and welfare services that once relieved some are bound to be restricted when they are most needed. And education, universally praised in Japan, will run short of funds.

When it comes to the workers, they will find it increasingly difficult to get by on wages that hardly improve even while certain expenditures, especially housing, continue swelling. More than ever, people will have to dip into their savings for ordinary expenses, further increasing their anxiety about the future. Meanwhile, since the consumers do not have much more to spend, many of the small firms and shopkeepers that live off them will find it harder than ever to survive.

As for the government, it will fall into a state of creeping mendicity. It is inevitable that some expenditures should rise. Merely the need to pay wages to civil servants, to keep up public buildings and facilities, and to meet minimal ongoing commitments require that. In particular, it will be necessary to find ever greater sums to pay back the old government bonds as they fall due. If taxes are not raised, the government will live from hand to mouth and have to turn to the banks to absorb more bonds and cover its endless deficits.

This means that, if the three old men have their way and there is no miraculous recovery abroad that allows Japan to expand exports as in the past, the economy will not revive. By adopting a policy of retrenchment at a time when stimulation was probably more suitable, it will have been slowed down artificially. And the Japanese can enjoy a life of "endurance" and austerity when it was probably not necessary.

PART THREE

REMEDIES

8
The "Sunrise" Industries

The Last Frontier

No country has a more enviable reputation for looking into the future and preparing for it than Japan. This is shown by its growing passion for the 21st century, which is still a rather remote horizon for other countries but seems to be almost the threshhold of many Japanese endeavors. And it is given substance by actual projects which are launched periodically to find and create new industries to replace present ones when they decline, part of the ongoing process of targeting.

In this manner, it is widely felt that Japan will continue catching up and then proceed to pull ahead of most of its competitors. It appears to be on the fast track to the wonder world of the future, one in which technology and knowledge-intensive industries will have supplanted labor and capital-intensive ones and in which people will finally relish the joy and comfort of a truly worthwhile life.

This thesis, which is very appealing to the Japanese and their admirers, does have a basis. The private sector has indeed been engaged in more than just a frantic dash to produce today's goods and pauses occasionally to consider those of tomorrow. Much of this chore falls upon Keizai Doyukai (Japan Committee for Economic

Development) which brings together the more dynamic and enlightened elements of big business. Back in 1979, it already issued a first report on the subject and followed that up with a second, more complete version, in 1982.

"Building an Industrial Structure for the 21st Century," the fruit of its labor, introduces eleven areas in which Japan must endeavor to play a leading role. These are to be its frontier industries. They are: biotechnology, computers and new electronics devices, telecommunications, lasers, industrial robots, engineering, urban development, aerospace, nuclear power, ocean development, and new materials.

In these sectors, Japanese companies must make every effort to move ahead. It is conceded, quite rightly, that the key to this will be enhanced research and development and graduation from copying and innovation to "independent high technology development." For such reasons, the Japanese have regularly increased their R&D expenditures over recent years, reaching an all-time high in fiscal 1982 of ¥6,529 billion. This represents 2.4% of gross national product and places it third after the United States and Soviet Union. Obviously not all of this went into the frontier sectors. But they are gaining an ever larger share.

Not surprisingly, in a country where government and industry cooperate closely, there has been considerable backing from the bureaucracy. The Ministry of International Trade and Industry undertakes its own studies of the future industrial structure and issues periodic reports. These coincide with the views of business circles as to where the emphasis should go because, among other things, businessmen sit on its committees. Even more to the point, the primary purpose of MITI is to serve industry.

To this end, in 1981, MITI adopted a ten-year plan

to spend some ¥104 billion on new generation technologies. While this may sound like a lot of money, it really is not so much when divided by ten years and then compared to the vastly superior amount spent by private companies. But it will play a crucial role because it is directed toward a narrow range of research topics, especially in the fields of new materials, biotechnology and new electronic elements.

Yet, despite all this, the going will be rough. A look at Keizai Doyukai's list will show that in some areas the Japanese are quite advanced, such as computers, industrial robots, and ceramics among the new materials. In others, they are just average competitors, such as nuclear power, engineering and urban development. And for some sectors, they are actually quite backward, like lasers, aerospace and ocean development.

It will take an unprecedented effort to make decisive progress in these frontier industries because, this time around, the more advanced partners may not be so willing to cooperate. Also, some of the products are extremely sophisticated or expensive and development costs will be enormous. Moreover, some of the products will be hard to sell on highly specialized and restrictive markets, like aircraft and nuclear power plants. Others are less suited to Japan, like undersea mining, or actually cost money, like urban development. Finally, a few have military applications, such as aircraft and lasers, and will be strongly subsidized by certain countries.

Yet, even if the Japanese do manage to find some hot commercial articles which can be manufactured and sold in large quantities, this is not the end of their travail. What is necessary to succeed in the 21st century will be not only some new products but enough to compensate for older ones which have seriously declined. That will not be easy. It would be necessary to sell extraordinary

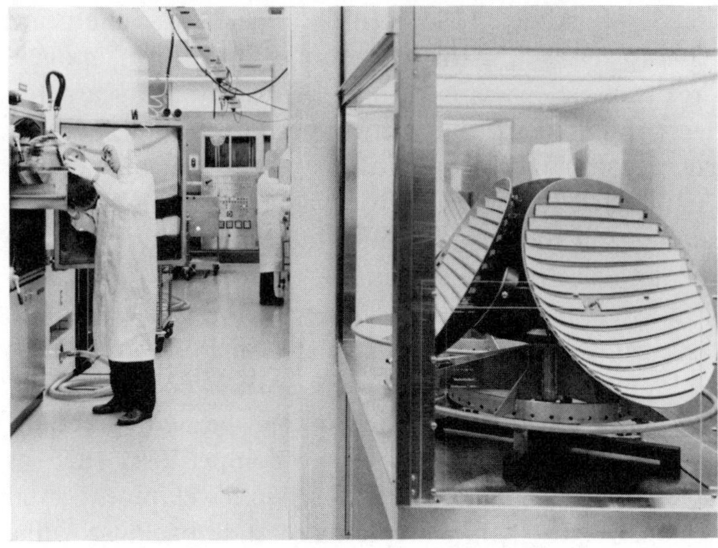

Exploring the brave new world of high tech.

Credit: IBM Japan

amounts of new materials or aircraft to make up for the expected slowdown of traditional materials or automobiles.

This is only made more difficult because some of the new products will actually undercut old ones and hasten their decline. Optical fibers will be replacing much larger amounts of copper wire for communications. New drugs developed through genetic engineering will replace old standards. Even video tape recorders, a rather ordinary electronic gadget by now, have contributed to a marked slump in sales of home movie cameras. This is an added reason for expressing concern as to whether the impulse from the "sunrise" industries will be great enough to counteract any slippage arising in the "sunset" industries.

Even if Japan is relatively well positioned for this lap in the industrial race, which it is in certain respects, the race will be harder than ever and not the sure thing some enthusiastic observers claim.

Creating "New" Materials

For almost a decade already, Japanese companies have been busily developing what is broadly known as "new materials." But it is only now that the Ministry of International Trade and Industry has decided to unify these efforts to create a "science of new materials." This shows rather clearly how the Japanese economy works, not so much through the vision of bureaucrats, as is commonly claimed, but thanks to the initiative of private businessmen. Not until they have gotten far enough to demonstrate real potential, and justify some additional support, does the government come in.

The idea of creating such a "science,"now a high priority task of the Agency of Industrial Science and Technology which is dependent on MITI, is more than timely. The field of "new materials" is both active and chaotic. There is no proper definition of what a new material is and the activities undertaken by the various companies and research institutes are anything but coordinated. There is certainly more overlapping and duplication than cooperation and a bit of organization would not hurt . . . as long as it does not deprive industry of its vital impulse.

The least that can be said about the "new materials" is that they are new and, one must assume, also better in certain ways than their predecessors. But the actual materials are of many different kinds. Some are metals, others plastics, yet others fibers, and the most numerous consist of ceramics. To call them "new" when the art of ceramics, or making simple metals, were invented many millenia ago makes little sense unless one is willing to concede that something has happened to raise them to such a high level that they really are a striking advance.

In the case of ceramics, which are variously known as "fine," "high performance" or "new," the differences are most impressive. Whereas traditional ceramics are made by taking natural materials, without high purity and in coarse grains, the new ones use artificially synthesized materials, of very great purity and fine grained. The old manufacturing process consisted of simple heat processing at normal atmospheric pressure. The new ones are produced under carefully controlled conditions often involving very high pressure and high temperatures. Rather than old standards like glass, cement or porcelain, one obtains products with intriguing possibilities.

The "new ceramics" boast rather extraordinary properties. They are often harder and stronger than metals. They resist heat and corrosion to an unprecedented degree. Some show good electrical insulation and others can be used as excellent semiconductors. They are much lighter than metals and less brittle than ordinary ceramics. In addition, they do not cause allergic reactions in the human body.

These characteristics naturally offer exceptional advantages for certain specific uses. The major one at present arises in electronics, where they serve as ceramic packages for IC chips. Somewhat more expensive than plastic packages, they bring higher performance and reliability. Since they are not rejected by the body, these ceramics can also be used for dental implants and artificial human bones. There are also a number of lesser uses for them as parts of solar cells, ball bearings for ball point pens, special scissors and knives and even artificial jewelry.

But the primary market of the future is likely to be "engineering" or "structural" ceramics, namely as parts and components of industrial machinery and equipment. Their use in automobile engines will be especially prominent. Due to their heat resistance, engines could reach much higher temperatures, making better use of the fuel, and also avoiding the cost and waste of coolers and radiators. Kyocera has already produced a ceramic engine for experimental purposes while Toshiba has a part metal, part ceramic prototype. Whole ceramic engines may only come into practical use in the 1990s. But well before that glow plugs, pistons, cyclinders and other parts will be common.

This is not to say that the "new ceramics" only have advantages. They still have some weaknesses and drawbacks and it will take years of patient research to overcome them. Although they are extremely hard, they do remain brittle and would break under excessive pressure. The breaking point would be much lower in the case of flaws and parts would not be reliable until such flaws could be avoided or at least identified through inspection, which is not yet possible. Alas, the new ceramics are also much more expensive than some of the conventional materials they should replace.

Another one of the "new materials" is titanium, a metal whose use had been rather restricted until now. It is exceptionally strong and lightweight, shows good heat and corrosion resistance, and can thus be used for certain special purposes. Among them are thermal exchangers of nuclear reactors, water desalination, chemical and pharmaceutical plants, and parts of aircraft engines. This has been enough to arouse the the interest of Japanese metal companies which have recently been boosting their production capacity.

In the long history of materials, plastics are pretty much of a newcomer. But they have already become so familiar that it would be surprising to talk of them as "new materials" if not for the occurrence of some interesting technological breakthroughs in this sector as well. The major difference is that, contrary to many common plastics that are relatively soft, some extremely hard types have been created. Most recently, a research team at Nara Women's University developed a polyethylene that was claimed to be unusually heat resistant and as strong as steel.

Such plastics could be used for entirely different purposes than the old ones. Aside from normal utensils and various household articles, they could be used as fabrics or even in construction to replace steel. That such possibilities are far from theoretical was proven stunningly by the latest Honda Ballade sports model. It shows superior running capability and fuel economy because more than 40% of the body is covered by plastic sheets. These are special "new" plastics developed by Honda and which could be applied by standard plastic injection on a mass production basis for the first time. This is just a step on the way to the wholly plastic covered car.

Carbon fiber is another of the rising new materials. It is extemely lightweight and yet terribly strong. But it was originally so costly that it could only be used for special products like aircraft. As production increased, and prices fell, it has come to be used in automobiles as well and also for sporting goods like golf clubs, fishing rods and tennis rackets. Japanese companies have taken a leading role in developing carbon fiber, with Toray presently the world's largest producer. It is followed by other big names like Toho Rayon, Mitsubishi Rayon and Kureha Chemical.

Now, however, carbon fiber may be overshadowed by boron fiber, whose mass production was only recently mastered by Vacuum Metallurgy, a relatively small company. The boron filament is claimed to be "stronger than carbon fiber and super-high tensile strength steel yet lighter than aluminum." It could be used for the space shuttle, military and commercial aircraft, and sporting goods, pretty much the same range as carbon fiber. And it could also compete in certain areas against steel or aluminum.

Even from these few examples, it must be evident that the "new materials" really are *new* in some very striking ways. They have made enough of an impression to be taken up by leading companies which have further refined and developed them. The market, for all of the new materials, has grown explosively. The new ceramics already reached the level of ¥350 billion last year and can be expected to sell over ¥1 trillion a year by the 1990s. The others are still smaller, but growing at incredible speeds. And this is happening at a time when most of the older materials are in the doldrums.

While Japan was rarely the originator of the "new materials," its companies were sufficiently far-sighted to realize their significance and enter the sectors quickly. In some cases, they have risen to the top, like Kyocera for ceramics and Toray for carbon fiber. And they can be expected to progress even more in the future. For the "new materials" are ideal for Japan. They require a highly educated research staff and skilled workforce and, what is even more noteworthy, they use existing raw materials more efficiently and even employ some of the few that this otherwise resource-poor country possesses.

Biotechnology Boom

There is no sector in which Japan's prospects for growth are nearly as good as in biotechnology. One reason is that the expansion here will be almost explosive. The other, less reputable but no less important, is that the Japanese are starting from ground zero and have nowhere to go but up.

Biotechnology, which uses living organisms or their components for industrial purposes, hardly existed in Japan not very many years back. Like so many other things, this field was pioneered in the United States and Europe. That is where the earliest research took place on cell fusion, plant molecular biology and genetics. That is where the recombinant DNA (rDNA) technique, the basis for genetic engineering, was introduced in the early 1970s. At that time, the Japanese only observed from a distance and engaged in little work of their own. Indeed, it was not until 1979 that the Japanese government adopted official guidelines on genetic research.

However, in the past few years, there has been a vir-

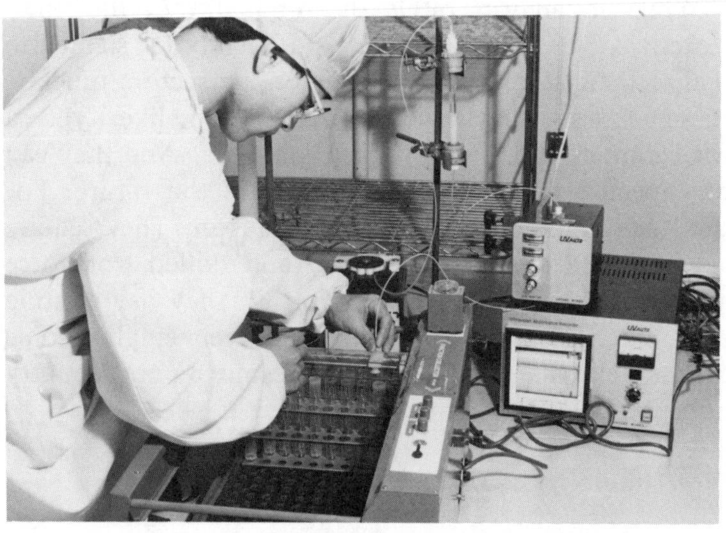

Joining in the biotechnology sweepstakes.

Credit: Hayashibara

tual stampede into biotechnology. This came from companies which saw great prospects in the sector and, at the same time, were concerned about the situation for their old activities. Many were pharmaceutical companies like Kyowa Hakko Kogyo, Takeda Chemical and Fujisawa. Others were in chemicals or petrochemicals like Sumitomo Chemical, Mitsubishi Chemical, Mitsui Toatsu Chemical and Asahi Chemical. There were also food companies like Ajinomoto, Suntory and Meiji Seika. And Toray came in from synthetic fibers.

By now there must be at least two hundred firms involved in one way or another in biotechnology, with more on the way. Even a cursory glance at the list will show that they include the biggest and the best of the Japanese industrial establishment. This makes the sector very different from what happened in the West where small entrepreneurial firms took the lead.

This means that the Japanese firms were able to move ahead more rapidly than otherwise. Endowed with abundant resources and large, trained staffs, it was possible for them to license many useful technologies or products so they did not have to start from scratch. In some cases, they actually went into joint ventures with top foreign biotechnology firms such as those between Mitsui Toatsu Chemical and Genex, Green Cross and Collaborative Research, Toray and Genentech.

Then they began pumping tremendous sums into their own research work in order to catch up. Their researchers were quickly shifted from other activities, went through a crash course in genetic engineering, and were soon assigned to crucial projects. When this was not enough, companies like Suntory scouted for Japanese researchers working in the field in the United States and recruited them. It was estimated that by 1982 the various firms were already spending ¥50 billion on R&D with the figures rising rapidly.

Better late than never, the government decided to help out. The Ministry of International Trade and Industry set up a Bioindustry Office. It launched a ten-year program involving key processes and costing some ¥26 billion. It talked the companies into forming a trade association to discuss common problems and avoid duplication. It also relaxed the regulations on genetic research to make things easier for the research workers.

So far, most of the Japanese thrust has revolved around the medical possibilities. This is normal since many of the participants are pharmaceutical companies and there is a huge potential market for the right drugs. The biggest drive has been to find a suitable anti-cancer drug and much of the effort is now concentrated on producing interferon. But other projects are studying biological response modifiers (BRM), tissue plasminogen activators (TPA) and monoclonal antibodies.

The second major interest is production of foodstuffs. Given their familiarity with fermentation and enzymes, Japanese firms have done very well. Ajinomoto developed an efficient method of mass producing amino acids by using rDNA technology. Kyowa Hakko Kogyo and Tanabe Seiyaku both found methods of mass producing ethyl alcohol by continuous fermentation. Even more revolutionary for a country like Japan, Morita Shokuzai, a small foodstuff maker, came up with a process that can reduce the time needed for making *shoyu* (soy sauce) from 6–8 months to a mere two weeks.

But this is still just scratching the surface of the wealth of possibilities opened up by biotechnology. The same techniques can be used in other sectors such as agriculture, chemicals, and energy. In the long run, it is expected that these sectors could become more significant than foods and medicine.

On the basis of their financial and industrial

capabilities, and with a little help from their foreign partners, the Japanese firms have been making very good headway. But it would be silly to believe the reports that they have already almost caught up with their American competitors, as is periodically claimed. The Japanese came in too late and this is a field where progress is extremely slow no matter how well endowed or ambitious a company may be. It is not unusual for a project to require ten years and more of fundamental research before any commercial product can be launched. And, according to Shukuo Kinoshita, president of Kyowa Hakko Kogyo, "we consider ourselves doing well if we succeed in one of ten research projects."

That is without really taking into consideration all the commercial risks. It is not only necessary to make crucial scientific breakthroughs and find a new product, it is also essential to manufacture it at an accessible price. So, the second step is to develop the right production techniques. Then, it is necessary to keep the quality better and the cost lower than anyone else who has been working on the same thing . . . and there may be many.

There is no better example of the risks of frontier technologies than the mad race to develop interferon which has attracted dozens of top biotechnology companies around the world, including about ten in Japan. There are already several firms which have succeeded in producing interferon by various methods, among them Takeda, Green Cross, Meiji Seika, Suntory and Kyowa Hakko. But one other rival, a relatively small one, Hayashibara has what is supposed to be the cheapest method and, if this is so, it could well corner the market.

Even then, it is assumed that interferon will not really be commercially available in large quantities until the end of the decade. In the meanwhile, other projects are being pursued on cancer breaking factor (CBF) which could replace it not long after. Then would come monoclonal antibody, which has a strong specificity to cancer. So, interferon might have a short lifetime despite the tremendous effort in developing it. Worse, it has yet to be proven that interferon will really be effective against cancer. Some scientists insist it is not suitable or could actually spread cancer.

Under such conditions, of the dozens who entered the race, only some ultimately succeeded in cultivating interferon. Of those, not many will be able to produce it cheaply enough to survive the competition. And they will have to make whatever money they can before the next, improved version of interferon, or some other drug, takes over. This shows the risks involved in spending huge sums on R&D. And they apply not only to interferon but just about every project that is undertaken in the challenging world of biotechnology.

Be this as it may, as far as most of the participants are concerned the stakes are certainly worth the effort and they will take whatever risks are necessary. The figures for future turnover of products that will be generated by biotechnology vary depending on the sources. But they are always stupendous. It is generally felt that the range would be from ¥4.2 trillion to ¥6.8 trillion in the year 2000 for Japan alone. Worldwide, it could be twenty or thirty times as much. This would make it a very big industry by any standards.

Information As Industry

Telecommunications, like most other sectors, is an industry of the past, the present and the future. For, it is a highly segmented industry in which literally thousands of different products are contained and each one of these products is continually undergoing change and improvement. This makes it, in certain ways, the ideal industry for the Japanese and they have thrown themselves into it with great energy.

Communications equipment in the narrow sense, your telephones, telegraphs and broadcasting gear, the switchboards, transmitters, receivers and the like regularly bring about a very large amount of production. The latest figures, those for fiscal 1982, added up to ¥1,168 billion. It is forecast by the Communications Industries Association of Japan that the output of such equipment should continue growing by about 10% a year and reach ¥1,901 billion in 1987. It would not be surprising if similar growth also continued into the next decade and beyond, as the industry steadily plods ahead.

But there are a number of other sectors which are closely related to telecommunications and which have assum-

A vision of comfortable living in the future communications society.

Credit: NTT

ed a vigorous life of their own. One, which is already quite familiar, will be increasingly important in the short term already. That is facsimile. Your standard facsimile has undergone incredible improvements over recent years. It is smaller, more efficient and cheaper. It can transmit in color as well as black-and-white. The transmission time was shortened radically and this also reduced costs which are partly related to use of transmission lines.

With this, sales have been expanding rapidly. The biggest expansion has taken place in Japan. Unlike Europeans and Americans who can easily send short or urgent messages, the Japanese are handicapped by use of *kanji* which cannot be transmitted by telex. But they can be sent over facsimile. Thus, the Japanese have been buying extensively. As their own models improved, exports have also caught on. Present sales are about ¥180 billion and they are expected to reach ¥500 billion by fiscal 1988.

There is an even more exciting product for the medium term. That is optical fibers whose use should revolutionize the whole field of telecommunications. Optical fibers can be made much thinner than ordinary copper cables, actually as thin as a hair, and they can carry large numbers of digital signals simultaneously. Even when many fibers are bundled together in one cable, there is no mixing of signals. Nor is there as much need for repeaters to carry signals over long distances.

Despite their superior technical characteristics, optical fibers are still more expensive than copper cables, considerably more so. But research is continuing to bring the cost down implacably and it should not be many years before optical fibers are both better and cheaper. Then there should be almost no limit to their potential. Even now, the prospects are rosy with sales rising above the ¥50 billion mark and expected to hit ¥250 billion a year by 1990. That is for domestic purposes. The international market would be considerably larger, and Japanese firms are well placed to get some of it.

For the longer term, the most prominent item is communication satellites as well as the earth stations and other related equipment. Here the picture is very different. Japan is not only far behind the United States, it also lags behind France and Germany. About two dozen satellites of one sort or another have been launched by Japan, but only a few of them are used for communications. Most notable are the CS-2 series, two of which were recently put into orbit. While showing good capabilities, they are relatively small and therefore only carry a rather modest number of channels (making each one proportionately more expensive).

Work is now proceeding on larger, more sophisticated satellites like the ETS-VI being designed by Japan's National Space Development Agency. It would weigh two tons and be ready for launching by 1992. But, even then, it would probably not be as large as American or European counterparts. Considerably more serious is the fact that, by producing in small series, it is impossible to bring costs down to a competitive level. Even the recent completion of a special plant by NEC, Japan's major builder, will not make a sufficient difference since it can only handle four satellites at a time. Thus, rather than turning the satellite business into a money-making proposition, it will probably continue absorbing subsidies.

In addition to the hardware, tremendous strides are being made in offering new services. The most impressive effort here is related to the Information Network System already under construction by Nippon Telegraph & Telephone. The basic idea is to unite the existing separate networks, namely telephone, telegraph, telex, data transmission and facsimile, in one system. This would be a unified, digital network. It would be carried increasingly by optical fiber cables. The whole, terribly ambitious program is expected to cost ¥30 trillion by the time it is completed in 1995.

Naturally, both the digitalization and the switch to optical fiber will take time, but it is hoped that gradually this system will cover the whole Japanese archipelago. A first step was to open an INS model system in Mitaka, a suburb of Tokyo, in 1982. In 1985, a similar model will be demonstrated at the Tsukuba Exposition. If successful, the system will be established in larger cities, then in the prefectural centers, and ultimately everywhere. Meanwhile, a chain of optical fiber cables will stretch all the way from Sapporo to Fukuoka, some 2,800 kilometers, to form the backbone of the INS transmission system.

Through this system, it would be possible to offer many services which are presently either unavailable or only accessible to relatively few users. Among them are digital telephone sets, a rather ordinary gadget, and digital sketch-phones, considerably more novel since they can carry voice and handwritten graphics. Facsimile will be accelerated and multi-media communications permitted by wiring various terminals to a single telephone line. Video conferences, connecting people in different places with television screens, can be held. And two-way television communication will spread.

One of the first, and most widely heralded steps, will be full-fledged introduction of NTT's CAPTAIN system. This is a videotex method similar to "prestel" in Britain and other systems in Europe and America. By using a keypad, subscribers can retrieve image frames on their own TV screens which will provide them with all sorts of information including news, stock market prices, sales at department stores, and so on. Going further, they will be able to purchase articles such as clothing, food or airline tickets through the system and also use it to pay utilities charges or credit card debts. Another wrinkle would be to transfer money in and out of bank accounts.

But these new services are not only of interest to the users and consumers, they are also creating an industry in its own right. People will obviously have to pay for some of the CAPTAIN equipment, even if they use their old TV set. They must at least get an adapter to link the TV to the telephone, now priced at about ¥100,000 and expected to decrease to about ¥50,000 later on. Subscribers will have to pay for receiving some information and for the use of telephone circuits. Those advertising their wares will pay as well. With satellite or cable television, special antenna or lines will be necessary. And new companies may go into business to provide the essential software. No one knows what all this will add up to, but it will not be negligible.

Thus, the information society, regarded as the cornerstone of Japan's brave new world in the 21st century, will not only make life cozier. It will also give a further impulse to the economy.

Delayed Take-Off

Back in 1980, when it was in a particularly bullish mood, the Ministry of International Trade and Industry proudly announced that Japan's aeronautical industry would be the biggest in the world by the 21st century. The aerospace companies were no less optimistic, predicting vast increases in sales. And journalists periodically exercised their poetic inspiration by writing about the "take-off" of the industry.

Alas, not that much was accomplished. During the late 1970s, production revolved around ¥250 and ¥290 billion. Finally, in 1981, there was some improvement, as output rose to ¥327 billion. When it actually jumped to ¥440 billion for fiscal 1982, there were renewed feelings of elation.

However, such feelings are certainly premature. While the showing was somewhat better, even ¥440 billion only made the aeronautical industry a rather modest one by Japanese standards. In any international comparison, it was actually quite puny. It only represented a third of the German industry, a fifth of the British or French industries, and a mere thirty-fourth of the American industry.

Moreover, there was no real reason to expect this progression to continue into the future and catapult the industry into a high growth trajectory. For, the improved sales figures were not part of a trend but simply the reflection of three major projects which happened to materialize at about the same time.

They consisted of production of two military aircraft, the F-15 fighter and the P-3C anti-submarine plane, both of which were manufactured in somewhat larger numbers but with no intention of expanding production further. The other project was participation in the production of the Boeing 767 whose orders have actually fallen.

This means that it is unlikely that there will be another sharp rise in the near future. With luck, output for fiscal 1983 will be ¥460 billion. And a slow upward, and sometimes downward, trend should continue for a number of years thereafter. Perhaps, by the end of the decade, there will be another step up, appreciable but not extraordinary.

It is not hard to make such forecasts for this industry because everything depends on the success of a small number of very large projects which take years to be launched and even more years to materialize. A look at the projects being mooted at present is just moderately encouraging.

First of all, it must be stressed that the mainstay of the Japanese aeronautical industry is military procurement. This accounts for a good 80% of total turnover. If more aircraft are ordered, the industry will do well. If not, it will be in difficulty. Given the increasingly tight budgetary constraints, which also apply to defense expenditures, there is no reason whatsoever to expect much progress on this front.

So, it is essential to develop some civilian projects if the industry wishes to grow. But that is not so easy. Japan, desite its tremendous industrial capabilities in other sectors, is still a novice here. It has only undertaken the production of one proper commercial airliner on its own. This is the YS-11, a 60-seater turboprop of which about 180 were manufactured from the mid-1960s to the late 1970s.

Rather than moving on to a bigger project, the Japanese were reduced to making some smaller aircraft. Mitsubishi has been producing the MU-2, which is a 10-seater turboprop, and the MU-300, a business jet. But production of the former was suspended recentiy and there are not many orders for the latter. Aside from that, some helicopters are being made, such as the BK-117 which is part of a joint production program between Kawasaki Heavy Industries and Messerschmitt-Belkow-Blohm.

This means that the commercial side is probably in worse shape than the military side. Yet, there are some projects in the offing which could make a difference.

For years, the Japanese have fondly caressed the idea of producing what is known as the YXX. This is supposed to be a 150-seater passenger plane which would

Aerospace: take-off of a new industry.

Credit: Foreign Press Center/Kyodo

be the key to future growth. However, rather than launch it on their own, the Japanese have negotiated with several different groups, including Boeing, McDonnell Douglas, Fokker and Aerospace for joint development. This has naturally slowed down any progress and made things a bit more complicated.

Boeing will probably be Japan's partner in this phase as well although other tie-ups may also materialize. This would be a step further than the 767 project for the participating firms, Mitsubishi Heavy Industries, Kawasaki Heavy Industries and Fuji Heavy Industries. Now they would share in the design, financing and marketing as well as the manufacturing. And their share will be raised to 25%. But it may not be until the 1990s that many of the new aircraft are produced.

Another project, which was mulled at length and has since grown into a major consortium, is the development of a new jet engine which would be suitable, of all things, for a 150-seater passenger plane. The program, which is estimated to cost $1 billion, is being undertaken by Japanese Aero Engines Corporation (consisting of Mitsubishi, Kawasaki and Ishikawajima-Harima Heavy Industries), Britain's Rolls-Royce, America's Pratt & Whitney, Germany's Motoren und Turbinen Union, and Italy's Fiat. The Japanese would handle about 23% of the total work and put up 20% of the capital (half of this apparently from MITI).

One last project must be mentioned, namely the work on a Short Take-Off and Landing (STOL) plane which was entrusted in Kawasaki by the National Aerospace Laboratory of the Science and Technology Agency. Initiated back in 1977, it has made commendable progress and the first flight of a prototype was made in 1984. But it will still take many more years for STOL aircraft to be produced commercially on any decent scale.

Aside from this there is a space industry including the production of rockets. So far most of them have been designed and built in cooperation with American companies and using many imported components. Early in 1984, it was decided that Japan should now go ahead on its own and produce an H-2 rocket capable of putting a two-ton satellite into orbit. By advancing the date for completion to 1990, the Space Development Council was taking a big risk since the technology was not yet ready. And there was also a financial risk since the project was expected to cost $900 million (assuming no overruns). Still, having committed their national pride, it is likely that Japanese rockets will be competing in space by the 21st century. The only drawback is that they will probably cost much more than they can possibly earn.

Thus, there is no doubt that Japan is on its way to becoming a major aerospace power. As in the past, it can certainly assemble the technology, accumulate the capital, and make the necessary effort. But, given the costs and the competition, this will have to be the biggest effort the country ever made, something beyond all comparison with what was done for automobiles or electronics.

9
Tackling The Tertiary Sector

Dawn Of The Post-Industrial Age

The tertiary sector is Japan's last economic frontier. Yet, despite all the talk of entering the post-industrial age, there does not seem to be much pioneering spirit around. Rather, like the worst Western models, the government prefers shoring up sectors that are bound to decline like agriculture and ailing industries. Businessmen continue flogging the same old products, and some few new ones, when all about them are unheard of possibilities for growth.

Nevertheless, the tertiary sector has been gaining ground over recent decades and will continue expanding in the future. That will arise partly from a pull as the Japanese realize just how much potential there is. Often the insight will come from foreign experiments or even foreign companies entering the market. But it is just as likely to arise from a push as the primary and secondary sectors shrink and managers there have to find new outlets.

To some extent, the tertiary is a residual into which everything left over from the other sectors, whatever is not farming, fishing, mining or manufacturing, is tossed. This gives it an extraordinary breadth of contents and makes it an almost endless source of opportunities.

It also makes any systematic handling of the subject a bit difficult.

Still, some major branches can be highlighted, such as distribution (wholesale and retail), finance (banking, securities, insurance, etc.), real estate, and the services more narrowly defined. Among these services, some are related to businesses, others to individuals, and yet others to social groups. In each of these areas, the potential will vary very considerably.

Distribution should, if anything, become a smaller share of the Japanese economy because it is still more complex and unwieldy than in most advanced countries. However, for this to happen, the older, less efficient firms will have to be replaced by more rational and productive ones. That is what revitalized the sector these past years as department stores, superstores, convenience stores, box stores and so on replace and gradually displace the earlier establishments. The process will certainly take another decade or more to complete.

In the field of finance, the Japanese often regard themselves as quite advanced. If notice is only taken of conventional banking, they are probably right. But there is a lot more to be done in leasing and insurance before they catch up with the rest. There is more room for leasing of not only plant and equipment but such commonplace things as car rental. Now that the population is aging, new types of policies and more insurance in general are needed. But even the banks are very remiss in lending to small and new firms or individuals. It is about time proper consumer finance companies replaced the crude *sarakin* operations and venture capital were mobilized.

Far more potential exists for real estate than many realize. Japan is one of the few countries where people are almost forced to buy a house or apartment rather

Evolving Sectoral Composition

	Share of GDP (%)			Share of Labor Force (%)		
	1970	1980	2000	1970	1980	2000
Primary	6.0	3.7	4.2	17.4	10.4	4.9
Secondary	43.1	38.2	31.5	35.2	34.8	33.3
Tertiary	50.9	58.1	64.2	47.3	54.5	61.8

Source: *Japan In The Year 2000*, Economic Planning Agency, 1982.

than rent it. This is expensive and inconvenient. It also creates special problems for those who move, have temporary transfers, or need bachelor's quarters before buying a family home. House and apartment rental already emerged decades ago in Europe and America. In Japan, it seems to be something that will only materialize toward the 21st century.

The greatest possibilities, however, lie in the services as such. Those directed toward businesses stand the best chances of advancing, since managers always find extra money if the new service will help. Now that the recession has discouraged companies from doing everything on their own, they may also want to use small service firms to fill the gaps. This can consist of consulting by accountants, auditors, architects, designers, engineers, lawyers or others in liberal professions. It could take the form of offices specialized in putting together computer systems, renting time on them, or providing software. There is plenty more room for less sophisticated operations as well, like print shops or delivery services. Advertising also seems bound to continue expanding.

In a recession, business tends to slump for many of the services related to personal wishes. Yet, surprisingly enough, even those services have been thriving in Japan. That is partly because not all the needs were met for ordinary things like laundries or bookshops. In other cases, new types replaced older ones, which explains the sharp rise in fast food places. But a shift in tastes, and increased earnings within certain categories, have resulted in a leisure boom which passed through numerous boomlets from pachinko to bowling, golf, skiing and now tennis. If the Japanese would finally obtain more free time, this is a branch of the economy which could really blossom.

It is not quite certain where to include the latest of many fads, the information revolution. The Japanese are now promised an information society which will affect both businesses and individuals. The former will become increasingly computerized. To benefit from this, they will want access to data banks and research institutes. They will also use new forms of communications, telex, facsimile, tele-conferences and so on. The public at large will also participate through the CAPTAIN videotex network, cable television, satellite broadcasts, and much more. Soon their homes will also boast computers (and later robots) that take over many of the daily chores.

The final service sector, including activities related to social groups, communities and even the nation as a whole, has not been expanding so rapidly. And, so far much of the expansion has concerned the young, such as baby care centers, kindergartens, and "educational" establishments which prepare youngsters for entrance exams. Much less growth has taken place in establishments catering to the aged, including special clinics, old age homes and the like. However, in the last few years, the shift has become noticeable as welfare facilities for this category increased four times as fast as the rest.

Just how far growth can go here is uncertain. It is partially a function of the demographic and health state of the nation. Since Japan is expected to have the most aged population in the world by the early 21st century, it would be normal to assume that huge amounts of people (numbering in the millions) will need medical care and hospitalization and similar amounts (again numbering in the millions) will end up in old age homes. According to reliable studies, to meet the mounting needs, the country would have to increase its medical expenditures twelve times over by the year 2025 and its spending on pensions would be sixteen times larger.

There is no other broad sector of the economy which could count on an expansion in the order of sixteen, or even twelve times, during that period. But the question arises as to whether these increases will actually be made, no matter how urgently they are needed. That is what makes this branch of the services so special. Much will depend on whether the government steps in to encourage the necessary growth or whether, as now, it tries to block the movement. Yet, even without government consent, people will age and fall ill and more money than ever will flow into the services that care for them. What does not come from the state will, in part, be paid for by those directly concerned. And the aged as a social category will dispose of sufficiently large resources to trigger a response among private entrepreneurs.

With so many opportunities arising, and the whole tertiary sector in a constant state of flux, it is hard to understand why more enthusiasm is not generated. Perhaps it is because the products here are more often "soft" than "hard" and therefore unfamiliar to existing companies. Worse, in Japan, the services have traditionally been regarded as less reputable and worthy than industry or even farming. But it would be an unwise businessman who lets too many chances go by.

The government is also aware of some of the potential. It has taken a fancy to the possibilities of an information society and the supposed "softnomization" of the whole economy. But it is the biggest obstacle to progress in the crucial sector of medical treatment and care for the aged. Because it is unable to raise the tax revenue it shuns the responsibility. Still, even the bureaucrats must realize that the needs will continue growing no matter what happens and the politicians must eventually grasp that old people can vote just as purposefully as young. In fact, if the aged were organized, they could easily outvote any other lobby.

Moreover, expansion in the tertiary sector, including services, is essential to keep the economy moving. More and more production will come from this direction and, even now, it accounts for 59% of gross national product. Equally important, it already employs 56% of the labor force. While it is somewhat less productive than the other sectors, it is clearly more successful at absorbing labor. With unemployment expanding rather than shrinking, and more people joining the ranks every year, this could be its greatest contribution to economic advancement.

Thus, after years of having fondly dreamed of entering the post-industrial age, the Japanese discover that this is not as simple as they thought. They find that there are both advantages and disadvantages and there are costs involved in certain gains. But this is no time to hesitate. That is why it is so important to adopt a more positive and intelligent approach than has been shown so far.

Creating A Real "Leisure Boom"

Ever since the early 1970s, Japan has apparently been ungulfed in a "leisure boom." It is played up in the press and television, publicity campaigns are launched by the firms selling goods, and the Japanese themselves have noted some welcome changes. There is also an increasing desire in official circles to convince the world that leisure has really caught on. This is necessary in order to shatter the embarrassing image of the Japanese as workaholics and prove that they are just ordinary people who know how to enjoy themselves like anyone else.

The government's interest was shown, among other things, by the creation of a Leisure Development Center by the Ministry of International Trade and Industry. While it does not develop much leisure, it certainly compiles statistics that make Japan look like one of the most progressive countries when it comes to participation in just about anything. According to it, about half the population engages in dining out, domestic sightseeing, driving about, playing cards and watching television.

It's not much, but we call it leisure.

Credit: Foreign Press Center/Kyodo

Nearly a quarter of the people are into things like bowling, calisthenics, baseball, jogging and swimming.

The amount of business generated by the booming leisure market is, it claims, no less than ¥40 trillion a year at present or roughly 15% of gross national expenditure. This would make it bigger than sales of steel, or automobiles, or electronics. Which is not surprising since, to embellish the statistics, it does not hesitate to make a rather broad definition of leisure. It includes sales of beer, whiskey and sake. Purchases of radios, televisions, VTRs, home movie cameras, and even personal computers are added. And, for good measure, even expenditures on jewelry and cosmetics are tossed in.

There is no doubt that the leisure market has been expanding rapidly, and people enjoy more such activities than before, but there are very few Japanese who would be so naive as to take these statistics at face value. They know that leisure, for the average worker or salaryman, is still just recovery from a grueling week's work and a chance to spend some time with the family or friends. That explains why so much of it is concentrated in watching television, puttering around the garden or repairing the house. A drive somewhere in the family car and lunch in a restaurant along the way are already a high point. Otherwise, time is spent playing pachinko, bowling, or practicing golf in a teeing range, all of which can be done in the neighborhood.

They also realize that, while millions engage in some of the more impressive activities, they are usually the same millions. Much of the sports are practiced by high school and university students, the latter boasting more free time than any other social category. Some housewives and young working women have since joined this rather small leisure class. But there is little room for your ordinary worker or salaryman . . . unless it is part of the company program. Then, they engage in calisthenics before work, eat and drink out with colleagues, play golf with customers, and dutifully appear for the annual picnic or excursion.

So, for all the millions of people involved and all the trillions of yen spent, the leisure industry is still in its infancy in Japan. It consists largely of what can be regarded as petty leisure, things that can be done on the quick, on the cheap, or by those few categories which have the time and the money. It is still a shadow of what passes for leisure in the West, and might be referred to as grand leisure. That implies more frequent practice of sports and hobbies, regular membership in sporting clubs or social groups, and enjoyment of substantial free time. This is also a leisure which, as the term should connote, is undertaken by the individual because he likes it and not accomplished at the behest of his school or company.

That Japan cannot possibly have such a grand leisure is immediately obvious from looking at the prevailing work schedules which show that the Japanese still put in many more hours than the inhabitants of other advanced countries. Actually, they work as much as 250–400 hours a year more than most Europeans and Americans. Many still do not have a two-day weekend every week and the official summer vacation merely runs into about two weeks. However, in practice, only about 5.5 days are taken at present.

This means that most men and many women simply do not have the time to engage in much leisure and what there is of it remains pretty petty. This naturally ties down their families to some extent, since the wives have to stick around the house and the children cannot even enjoy their considerably longer vacations. Most of them spend the summer studying rather than playing or attending summer camp. Thus, aside from some narrow and rather special groups, most Japanese only partake marginally of the tremendous possibilities that exist.

While regrettable, that does at least indicate that there is vast potential to create a grand leisure in Japan, one similar to that in the West. The major emphasis would have to be on benefiting from longer vacations, in the summer and conceivably also winter, as well as regular weekends and some extended holidays. The basic thrust would be to get the Japanese out of the cities, where all too many of them spend too much time, and into other parts of the country, especially the more remote countryside, which they hardly know.

Japan's edge on long hours worked in industry only grows.

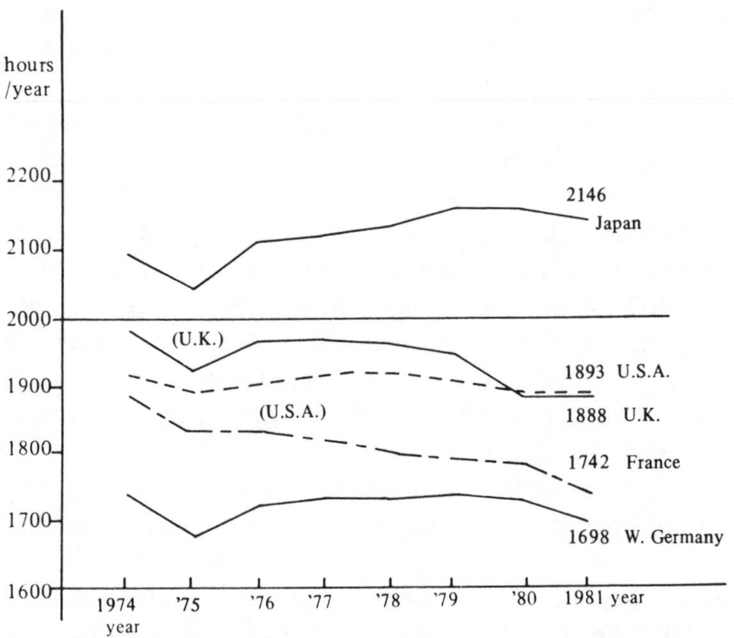

Sources: *Monthly Labor Statistics Survey* for Japan, *Labor Costs in Industry* for EC, *Bulletin of Labour Statistics*, ILO, etc.

There, away from the hustle and bustle of city life, and its shallow culture many are addicted to, the Japanese could undertake various activities with their families or friends. This might include hiking and mountain climbing, touring and sightseeing, and any number of sports that require more space, like golf, tennis, swimming, sailing and so on. Or they might just read a good book or engage in their favorite hobbies. For once, they could also commune with nature. There is no need for the activities to be spectacular, or excessively costly, as long as they permit a chance to do what one wants and finally unwind.

Economically, such a move could contribute immensely to the growth of a real tourist industry. It would result in the establishment of hotels, inns, vacation centers and so on. They would soon be accompanied by restaurants, coffee shops, and quick food joints. Sporting facilities and shops would doubtlessly follow. There might also be summer camps and day care facilities for the children. All of this would generate business. More important than the sums involved, however, would be the fact of reviving these country areas which have veen decaying and losing population for years but would be the ideal site for a vacation.

Socially, this would almost be a revolution. It would bring families together under different, and more congenial circumstances, enabling the father/husband who is often away to get to know his children and wife. It would permit encounters among young people of both sexes without need for a go-between. And it would create meeting places for Japanese of diverse regions and professions who might otherwise never see on another. The individual, family, and nation would gain, probably to the detriment of the most sacred institution, the company.

However, to bring about such a revolution, it will be

necessary to impose certain changes. That the Japanese want more leisure and are more dissatisfied with their meager allotment than people in any other advanced country, has already been recorded by numerous surveys. But they have to stop complaining that they would not know what to do with more free time or could not afford real leisure. Just like others before them, they will find more than enough to do and manage to put aside the money. The ways can be found once the will is there.

By now, it has been duly noted by the national authorities that the other advanced countries are seriously aggrieved by the long hours worked in Japan. The Ministry of Labor, which is most directly concerned, actually launched a plan to reduce annual working hours to less than 2,000 by 1985. This should be accomplished by reducing overtime and making full use of paid holidays. The trade union federations have also come out strongly for shorter working hours. And, it seems reasonably fair that, if the employers are not willing to increase wages, they could at least decrease the amount of work.

But it will still be necessary to convince the employers. They are the ones who have repeatedly dragged their heels on shorter days, two-day weekends and longer vacations. They even coerced their personnel into returning half of the paid holidays already granted. Thus, little will be achieved unless the workers and employees defend their gains and take their due. For this, the government will probably have to introduce particularly strong administrative guidance and, if that fails, take penal action.

Even then, it will require continuing external pressure to convince Japan that it can afford, and would be wise, to permit more leisure. Once started, however, there is little doubt that the Japanese will find it to be one of the finer Western innovations and something which fills a need. This could also mark the birth of a real leisure industry, one which would offer the people a happier and more fruitful life and solve some nagging social and economic problems on the way.

The One Sure Product—Housing

If there is any product which all Japanese eagerly desire, and for which there has traditionally been a very strong demand, then it is housing. The reasons are easy enough to grasp. Japanese people have a tremendous urge for their *own* home, one that belongs to them, preferably a small house in the suburbs but increasingly also a nice apartment in town. Crushed by business and social contacts in their daily life, they need a refuge, a place they can retreat to in the evening or on weekends.

In addition, as everyone must know by now, many Japanese are not satisfied with their present premises and would gladly change. Even according to the government's none too generous definition of suitable housing, about 14% of the existing dwellings are substandard. Anyone coming from the West would assume that the figure is much higher. Even the Japanese themselves regularly complain about it. The worst gripe is that there simply isn't enough space in the "rabbit hutches." But many are also poorly built, without adequate amenities, and sometimes not enough sunlight or silence.

It is things like this that made the construction industry one of Japan's largest and most dynamic. Year after year, it built new houses and found a never-ending demand for more. And it continued employing large numbers of people and making a major contribution to the country's gross national product. In 1980, however, something totally unexpected happened. The demand dried up and, for the first time in twelve years, housing starts dropped from the level of 1.5 million units a year to a mere 1.2 million units. Since then, the market has remained very sluggish and housing construction is still down.

What is even more amazing is that there are literally thousands of exceptionally attractive units that have been built and cannot be sold. Everywhere, in the newspapers, in subway ads, even in the more costly television commercials, there is publicity to sell some of these ideal homes. Salesmen even go from door to door to look for potential buyers. Yet, they cannot be sold. And, until they are, it will be hard to stimulate new building.

How could this happen? The answer is quite simple. In a time of stagnant earnings, the cost of housing continued rising at a considerable clip and now it is just too expensive for many families. For example, even a modest house in the suburbs, some 90 minutes from central Tokyo, will cost about ¥30 million. The typical buyer is a company employee in his thirties, with a wife and kids, earning about ¥3 million a year. Since he cannot afford this from his wages, he must take out a loan. It is not at all unusual for such families to devote a quarter of their budget to this expenditure. And they are being squeezed out of the market.

What can explain these infernal costs?

For one, there is the land price. The cost of land has been rising at an unprecedented rate ever since the war, especially in the larger cities. In fact, since 1955 the increase was over forty-fold in general and sixty-fold for places like Tokyo and Osaka. This has made the price of land among the highest in the world and, when building, a disproportionately large share of the total cost is paid for land. Meanwhile, the cost of construc-

Can't Japan do better than this? Housing is still a national shame.

Credit: A. Tsuchiya

tion itself has increased considerably, although far from the same rate as land.

But a further element cannot be overlooked . . . collusion. Land prices rose as fast as they did because of absolutely incredible land speculation that occurred during the 1960s and 1970s. This was engaged in not only by the original landowners or small time speculators but Japan's biggest and proudest companies, all of which have a real estate subsidiary and also bought land to profit from the expected price rises. There was doubtlessly also an understanding between the real estate agencies and the construction companies to see that they got a proper return. For, despite the extraordinary glut of housing at present, the prices have not fallen as they did in other countries.

Things are now in an impasse. The price of land and

housing is stabilzing, but not coming down. Buyers are doubtlessly interested, but not yet able to enter the market. There is little expectation of an upswing in the industry over the short them. And, even in the long term, unless something can be done to make housing more affordable, one of the most popular commodities will not be playing its role in the economy.

Yet, it would not be all that difficult to improve the situation. There is little hope that the land speculators or real estate agents will accept a modest loss. But other things can be done.

First of all, the land that does exist—even at the record-breaking price it commands—can be used much more wisely. Despite the extensive urbanization, most Japanese cities allow the spread of small, one-story, one-family houses when there is a crying need for larger units that make better use of the land. In fact, the recent trend has been in the wrong direction, toward what are called mini-developments. With proper zoning laws and building codes it should be possible to encourage more high rise and multi-story buildings so that more people can live on the same amount of land and the cost can be shared between them.

In addition, while modernization and rationalization have taken place in all other industries, construction has remained amazingly backward. It looks as if about every building were designed separately and built to order. There is very little standardization or prefabrication. In fact, for the dinky homes that sprout on the mini-developments, the techniques used look almost medieval, with carpenters crawling along the roof and doing most of the work by hand. Here, too, there is plenty of room for more efficient and cost-saving methods.

These various improvements, which should not be beyond the capabilities of the Japanese government and construction companies, would be able to bring down the cost of housing radically even in the rather unfavorable environment that prevails. If that were done, more people could buy the home of their dreams or at least something better than what they have now. The units that already exist might be bought up. And then it would be possible to increase the number of new starts as well. This would certainly make more Japanese happy than putting the same effort into boosting exports.

10
Paying For Growth

Exporting For Peace And Profit

For most international crises there is no quick fix. But for one of Japan's most painful problems, the unending succession of trade conflicts, there most definitely is. The Japanese could help their trading partners, and help themselves, quite simply by raising prices and seeking profits.

Anywhere else in the world, such advice would not even have to be given. In Japan, it may appear almost revolutionary. The reason few Japanese companies think of this is that they work on the basis of market share rather than profit. And, to expand their market share, they will gladly sacrifice profit in the short or medium-term and, if they are not lucky, sometimes in the long-term as well.

What foreign countries object to are not Japanese exports as such. They admire the quality and workmanship of Japanese televisions, video tape recorders, automobiles, steel, and so on. They do not object to the prices either, since they are usually quite modest for the product. What they do object to is being overwhelmed by these exports when they are sold in such large quantities that they create repeated surges and "torrential" flows.

There are various ways of decreasing the flow of exports, some more palatable than others. One is for the Japanese to exercise restraint, voluntarily or more likely under orders from the Ministry of International Trade and Industry. Another is for the foreign countries to get so angry that they clamp down restrictions. A final method, which has not been tried, is simply to raise the prices of their exports.

The economic logic behind this is flawless. Anyone with the slightest knowledge of how economies function or merely a feel for how people make purchases will realize that as the price increases the number of units sold decreases. When the price increases beyond a certain point, the total sales will also decrease as buyers find the product too expensive.

By following the supply and demand curve carefully, the Japanese can attain whatever point they want. If it is only wished to decrease the quantity sold, for example, fewer Japanese automobiles so more American ones have a chance, the price can be raised enough that fewer Americans will buy. But it need not be raised so much that there is a massive rejection of Japanese cars. If it is necessary to overcome a basic trade imbalance, which is quite another matter, then perhaps the Japanese would raise it even higher and make Japanese cars a sort of luxury.

Whenever Japanese businessmen hear about raising prices, they immediately get nervous. They insist that fewer units will be sold at higher prices. They are perfectly right. But, in this case, that is the goal! If they wish to avoid trouble with their trading partners, they must decrease sales. And, if they do not do that on their own, they will risk protectionist measures that will take the sales away from them anyway.

Those measures, however, are purely negative. They

take away sales and give nothing in return. Losing sales by raising prices has a good side, namely higher profits. It must be obvious that adding 10% or 20% to the price tag of any article costs nothing, you just put in another number. But this increase in price by 10% or 20% means a much larger increase in profit. For the sake of argument, if we assume that the original profit margin was 10% this addition would double or triple profit.

This profit could then be brought back to Japan and channelled into the domestic economy in various ways. It would, first of all, result in higher taxes which would feed the national budget and permit more public works. It might even sop up the deficits and enable the government to fulfill its own economic functions more effectively. It would also flow into further investment by the companies and higher wages for the workers. This latter would permit a resurgence of consumer spending and really get the economy moving.

It is obvious that reduced sales in quantity (fewer automobiles sold if not necessarily smaller total sales) would have some adverse effects such as less need of new plant or some unemployment. But certainly the massive increase in earnings would make it possible to employ people in other sectors and undertake other investments as the economy revives. Here, one could think of no better candidate than more housing construction.

The problem is, how does one convince the Japanese businessmen to look for profit? That really seems to go against the grain, although, during the recession, some of them have learnt the advantages of being solvent and keeping cash flow strong. And, even if they wished to raise their own prices, they would be worried about their competitors who might take advantage to win market share away from them.

This means, alas, that it might be necessary for MITI

to intervene. Still, if this were necessary, there is no doubt that it could do the job. It has set up countless anti-recession cartels as well as export cartels to share out the quotas for textiles, televisions or automobiles. There is no reason it could not take similar action here except in an earlier stage, this time to prevent protectionism rather than implement it.

The other alternative, this one no less strange to the thinking of Japanese managers, is to raise wages. If wages were raised a bit more, then the costs would also be a bit higher, and it would be essential to raise the sales price somewhat to make the same old profit. These higher prices would then have the desired effect of decreasing exports and the side effect of fueling the domestic economy.

This sort of reaction also has a solid base in economic theory. Higher wages, even more directly than tax rebates, channel additional purchasing power into the masses of the population and permit them to buy more. This gives a much needed stimulus to consumption and from there to production. If the impetus is sufficient the whole domestic sector could be revived.

But, many Japanese will object, these measures have already proven themselves to be defective in foreign countries because they lead to lazy managers who think only of profits and greedy workers who demand excessive wages when it would be better to increase productivity. The reply is "yes," that is true when these measures are pushed to an extreme.

But no one is asking the Japanese to exaggerate. The price rises or wage hikes need only be large enough to accomplish the desired goal. There is no intention of overdoing them and, given the reluctance of business circles, little chance that they could be overdone. If used with moderation these methods might work. Japan would admittedly lose some of its competitive edge, but certainly not all, and what is needed today happens to be a less—not a more—dynamic export sector.

Whether appealing or not, the Japanese economy has clearly reached a point where the old, tried-and-true methods not only do not work, they have become dangerous. It is time to look for something else and this is a good direction to look.

Getting More By Giving More

The Japanese economy is getting back in swing. From month to month, exports have been increasing and Japanese goods are again flooding foreign markets. The businessmen are happy because they are producing more. The government is happy because growth has finally accelerated. Only the foreigners appear unhappy because they cannot sell as much to Japan.

For 1983, Japan achieved the biggest trade surplus in its history, $20 billion. This is a vast improvement over the paltry $7 billion last year and even above the previous record of $18 billion in 1978. But it is already forecast that next year's trade surplus could well be two times as high.

This would be wonderful . . . if only the Japanese could figure out what to do with all the money they are earning. Some of it can be used to pay back past debts. Another portion can be used to purchase foreign securities or invest abroad. But Japan's needs would seem to be limited since a lot of it is simply accumulating in the gold and foreign exchange reserves.

With about $25 billion in reserves, a figure which could easily double and triple in the coming years, Japan will soon have the largest reserves in the world. They will not only be large in absolute terms. They will be hopelessly large in any practical sense since the main purpose of holding reserves is to cover trade deficits. And, if Japan keeps on exporting more than it imports, it has no use for this.

What then should Japan do? Its factories have been running flat out to produce more, its workers have been putting in overtime to augment the flow, and its traders have been busy selling the goods. Yet, all they have in return is bloated reserves.

If at least you could eat foreign exchange, perhaps with a bit of soya sauce, then things would be much better. Or, if you could build houses of gold like the Incas. Or perhaps it would be possible to make fashionable jackets of greenbacks or, for the ladies, French francs.

But none of this is feasible. Gold and foreign currency, beyond the reasonable needs of security, have absolutely no value unless they are exchanged for things that people really do need. This means things like raw materials, of course, so that Japan can produce more exports and fuel its own economy. But it also means things like beef and citrus fruit, or foreign manufactured goods, or long vacations abroad.

Unless the Japanese can find things to buy with their vast reserves, they will just be wasted. Indeed, worse than wasted, they will become a terrible curse for Japan.

This can hardly be avoided. The economic laws are implacable. If a country exports more than it imports, there will be a great demand for its currency which will appreciate sharply. When the yen rises, this makes it harder to sell Japanese goods abroad and thus exports slow down. It is also easier to import foreign goods because they are are cheaper, so imports rise . . . unless they are blocked.

Fortunately there is an automatic balancing mechanism

in the international economic system, because there is obviously none in the minds of Japanese businessmen or officials. This tends to rectify the excesses of exports every now and then when they cannot be borne by the rest of the world.

And, if this natural mechanism works too slowly, most foreign countries have found other ways of expediting the process. With an $18 billion deficit with Japan for 1983, and perhaps twice as much coming, the United States can do nothing else than restrict imports while waiting for the dollar to weaken. With a $10 billion deficit, the European Community is bound to do the same, only much faster.

So the only thing the Japanese can obtain from all this worthless money they are earning now is a yen that is much more costly. When this happens, the securities its people have bought will be worth less. The reserves they have painfully accumulated will also be worth less in terms of the yen. And they will wish they were not stuck with so much of the precious stuff.

Meanwhile, as happened back in the early 1970s and again in the late 1970s, when the Japanese were so foolish as to export too much, the yen will rise relentlessly. There is no telling how far or fast it will rise. But the last two times there was a sudden swing upward of about 30% followed by a slower sinking to some 20% above the previous prevailing rate.

This inevitably means that all Japanese goods will cost 20% or 30% more to produce and sell to foreigners. This will stymy exports very seriously and set the businessmen to thinking about how they can cut costs. The government will also get worried because the economy will slow down. And the population as a whole will worry that without exports the poor Japanese islands may sink under the sea.

If it's too expensive, why not import more Mr. Prime Minister?

Credit: Foreign Press Center/Kyodo

So, businessmen, officials and people will work like mad to rectify the situation. They will pull in their belts, they will accept wage restraints and put in extra hours, they will go without many potential imports. They will scrimp and sacrifice so that Japan can export more.

To what end? Well, obviously so that Japan can record new trade surpluses, so that more gold and foreign exchange can accumulate in the reserves, and so that—once again—foreign countries will restrict its exports and the yen can appreciate thereby initiating a new cycle.

It is well known that many swimmers drown because they insist on fighting a current that is too strong for them when they could very well have survived by floating with the tide. That seems to be Japan's fate. Its obsession for exporting repeatedly leads to disaster.

Yet, the solution is so easy. And Japan's own progression could be so much smoother and more fruitful. It just has to learn that trading is a matter of give-and-take.

There is no point to exporting if one does not import. There is no point to earning money if one does not spend it. If Japan would only open its market, and take in the products of others, it would be able to sell far more than otherwise without the frantic efforts it goes through now and which hurt as much as they help.

Why Can't Workers Earn More?

Ever since the traditional growth stimulus of exports has been sapped by mounting protectionism, Japan's economy has been stymied. It has proven impossible to switch to the normal source of growth the world 'round, namely domestic demand. This is surprising since personal consumption accounts for over half of gross national product or more than three times the level of exports. But it has simply been unfeasible to get people to buy much more than before.

With a huge population of 120 million apparently affluent consumers, it might be assumed that there should be no great difficulty in augmenting sales. Yet, despite official pronouncements of the government and tireless sales campaigns by the manufacturers and retailers, business has remained slack and any improvement has been marginal.

It is a bit pointless to ask, why? Everybody in Japan already knows why. The income of the average worker has been rising more slowly with each passing year. The formal wage hikes gained by the *shunto* keep falling, reaching a low of 4.4% last year. After subtracting inflation, hardly anything remains. According to the Ministry of Labor, the average real pay increase only came to a meager 1.6%, the worst showing in over a decade.

Meanwhile, due to bracket creep, wage-earners are paying more taxes than ever. The recent phony tax cut is not going to change that and the new indirect taxes will cut even deeper into disposable income. With less money to spend, quite naturally, people spend less and consumption fails to grow.

There is only one way out of this fatal spiral which keeps depressing the economy, and that is to increase wages more generously. Alas, in this country which is famed for management's care and concern with the lot of the worker, there is just one thing that companies are not willing to concede . . . more money.

Management, most visibly in the form of the Japan Federation of Employers' Associations or Nikkeiren, incessantly argues that the worst possible thing at present would be to boost wages. That would only lead to more inflation. Worse, it would reduce Japan's competitiveness abroad and make it harder to sell the exports on which the nation's salvation supposedly depends.

Nikkeiren has therefore reconfirmed its unwavering faith in the principle that wage hikes should be limited to the level of productivity rises. Back in the 1960s and early 1970s, when the increases in productivity were huge, this principle was not quite as prominent. But it has become nearly sacred now that productivity growth is relatively small.

Thus, management has proceeded from proposals that the annual wage increase be kept below 6%, to 5%, and then 4%, and now talks of granting only the automatic raises of 2% or 3%. For, in their heart of hearts, what the managers want has already been intimated by the three old men who run big business, Toshiwo Doko, Yoshihiro Inayama and Bunpei Otsuki. Their preference goes to a "zero increase."

While low productivity may provide an argument for suggesting low wage hikes, it is not really productivity that determines what wages can be safely given. That can only be derived from the competitive situation, especially for Japan's exports. As long as Japanese goods continue to sell for less than foreign goods, there is definite leeway to pay Japanese workers more. Given the considerable price margins most Japanese exports enjoy, there is actually a fair amount of room for improvement.

Just about all the statistics on comparative wage levels, aside from those concocted by Japanese management, show that the Japanese workers are still getting less than their direct Western rivals. And the gap is particularly big in export sectors. According to *Businessweek*, Japanese steel workers were earning $10.18 an hour compared to $11.51 for Germans and $22.74 for

Americans. Japanese autoworkers were earning a mere $7.22 an hour as opposed to $12.94 for Germans and $19.43 for Americans.

In such a competitive situation, there would be no danger in giving workers in these sectors an immediate wage hike of 10% or 15% and as much as their foreign counterparts in successive years. Similar wage increments could also be offered to workers in supplier and subcontractor firms. This would apply not only to steel and automobiles but most export industries, including electronics, machinery and high tech in general, since the margins are sufficiently wide there as well.

Admittedly, wages are not the only thing that goes into production costs. If, for some reason, American or German workers were paid more because their facilities were more modern or efficient, such a policy would be risky. But the fact of the matter is that Japanese steel mills, automobile plants, electronics factories and so on are vastly more productive than counterparts anywhere. They also use proportionately less labor. This means that even a 25% "bonus" would be far from suicidal.

If workers in these industries, which are the backbone of the economy, could be paid more than at present, they would obviously be able to consume more than at present. They would be able to buy any number of products from local industries which do not export, items like food, clothing, housing, entertainment and so on. This would make money circulate throughout the economy and help revive it. Indeed, in this way, domestic demand could finally become the driving force it should be.

In so doing, there might be some increase in inflation. However, it would not be all that much because the biggest wage hikes could be absorbed in higher prices for export goods and it would be the foreign buyers who bear the costs. Also, as for wages, inflation is comparative. The rates in Japan are still enough lower than abroad that some slight increment would not be disastrous.

But there is little chance that management would accept such a counter-argument. Japan's corporate leaders have gotten where they are by keeping wages in line during the 1950s, the 1960s, the 1970s and now the 1980s. They are already very old men, strongly set in their ways. They see no reason to modify their practices simply because the economic situation has changed radically in the meanwhile.

Moreover, top managers have another passion which goes much deeper than any concern for the workers. That is to endow their factories with the most efficient machinery imaginable so as to rationalize production and bring prices down further. When it comes to investment in plant and equipment, the reaction is almost the exact opposite of that for remuneration of workers. The desirable limit is almost infinity.

Japanese companies are always eager to buy more machinery and to automate their factories as much as possible. Although they are already well ahead of their American and European competitors, that is not enough. They now rush into computerization and robotization, spending vast sums of money whether it is necessary or not. This money has to be taken from somewhere, and the most convenient place is wages. So, the supposedly cherished workers suffer in two ways, their wages cannot be increased and some lose jobs to the new machinery.

Ever since the postwar economic drive began, Japanese companies have been plowing more money into plant and equipment. Investment levels, at over 30% of gross national product, are far higher than in the West where

20% is considered admirable. The average age of Japanese installations is about 8 years over against 15 year abroad. Japan is, if anything, overcapitalized. This means that the more advanced companies could easily put more money into wages and less into equipment.

So, there is a definite potential for switching from the old policy of sweating labor to keep costs down to a more intelligent and enlightened policy of paying workers a bit more because, in addition to producers, they are consumers. This realization, and such measures, would enable them to play the role and stimulate the economy. But it would require a new approach from company executives and government officials and there is reason to fear that they are too old and stubborn to learn new tricks.

11
Reforming Adminstrative Reform

Backward-Looking Reforms

A national magazine recently upgraded the highly touted administrative reform to a "revolution." If it is carried out, it might almost deserve that title when seen on the background of Japanese politics. This is far from the first attempt to rationalize and simplify the governmental structure. But it is the first one that looks likely to succeed to some degree.

The plan, which was submitted in March 1983, is the work of the Second Ad Hoc Commission on Administrative Reform. The first Ad Hoc Commission, which was active some eighteen years ago, accomplished little. Meanwhile, there have been repeated complaints about inefficiency and waste, and many other plans. None of them were implemented and some never even reached the stage of formal presentation.

That we have gotten this far, and that the Nakasone Cabinet not only accepted the report but made administrative reform one of the basic cornerstones of its policy, is a sign of the times. Japan could afford a more bloated bureaucracy during the period of rapid growth. Now that growth has slowed down considerably, and both businesses and private citizens are feeling the pinch, there is much more insistence on tax monies being used well.

It is also a reflection of the prominent role played by the Chairman of the Ad Hoc Commission, Toshiwo Doko. Doko, long head of the Japan Federation of Economic Organizations, known as Keidanren, enjoys exceptional prestige in business and government circles. And the very creation of the body arose from strong resentment in the business community, especially in big business, that the government was not doing its share at a time of economic hardship. Rather than ask for more taxes, it should slim its own services and become more efficient!

The work of the Ad Hoc Commission, which was unusually comprehensive in scope, has already been commented upon amply in the press. Most attention has been

Doko submitting the administrative reform to Suzuki and Nakasone.

Credit: Foreign Press Center/Kyodo

paid to the spectacular decision to turn three major public corporations over to private management. They are the Japanese National Railways, Japan Tobacco & Salt Monopoly, and Nippon Telegraph & Telephone. But this is just one of many aspects that were touched upon. The various sub-committees also made important recommendations concerning education and health care, land and housing, social security and the tax system. It looked into other government bodies as well.

While more interest was obviously focused on what was done, it must be admitted that some rather crucial chores were left undone. Although condemning higher taxes, no explanation was provided as to how to make up for existing revenue shortfalls, which seem to be growing. Although the three public corporations were dealt with extensively, and some smaller agencies were to be amalgamated, the reports were painfully silent about the core of the central government, the various ministries. They were simply asked to put their own house in order.

If the administrative reform plan is truly "revolutionary," then it is bound to arouse a degree of resistance. This is found in some business circles, but more so among the opposition parties, notably the Japan Communist Party, the Japan Socialist Party and Komeito. There are naturally objections from the trade unions in general, particularly the leftist Sohyo federation, and of course members of the JNR. There is also a sprinkling of complaints from certain social groups.

Nevertheless, the chances of a reform being implemented in one shape or another are rather good. The main reason is that so much of the population is in favor. Most business associations have stated their support of the Commission's plan and most factions of the ruling Liberal Democratic Party have agreed to back it. As for Prime Minister Nakasone, he repeatedly promised "to promote administrative reform with unrelenting resolve."

Thus, within the context of the administrative reform, the situation seems rather positive. The recommendations have been submitted, accepted, and are edging toward formal legislative approval and then implementation. People look forward to the relief this will bring in terms of lower taxes—or, more likely, smaller tax hikes—and greater efficiency within the government. Just in case, the budget is being kept under strict control.

The only serious question is, what if the context was too narrowly defined? This question is hardly ever raised. Indeed, some will wonder how anything could be wrong with such a noble cause as "small government." Yet, when one considers the broader economic situation, there are very definite grounds for criticism of what is being done.

Japan's most urgent problem at present is not "big government" but an exceptionally sluggish economy. From over 10% a decade ago, the growth rate has fallen to some 3% or 4%. This is largely due to the worldwide recession and restrictions on Japanese exports. Therefore, the only way out for the moment is to stimulate domestic demand.

This has been done in various ways in the past. The most effective was by running major public works programs. By putting up basic infrastructure and other large projects, it was possible to support the construction industry and also to employ vast numbers of workers. With the policy of budgetary restraint, part and parcel of the administrative reform effort, it has been necessary to keep public works expenditures down. So, one form of stimulation is ruled out.

During the present slump, it is actually small and medium-sized enterprises which are hurt most. They are generally weaker to begin with, sometimes excessively dependent on subcontracting, and usually short of credit. To make up for these inherent disavantages, the government usually provides special assistance to small businesses. This has also remained stagnant, ruling out a second source of stimulation.

Admittedly, the government budget is not growing as fast as before, although it is not being kept to "zero growth" as is sometimes claimed. This means that ordinary taxpayers, and especially corporations, are being assessed less than otherwise. But they are still paying more than before due to "bracket creep" arising from inflation. No matter how successful the administrative reform may be, there is not the slightest chance that taxes can actually be reduced. So, even a successful conclusion precludes this sort of stimulation.

This means that, although it was certainly not intended, administrative reform is getting in the way of economic recovery. This will explain why even certain business circles are at most lukewarm while the trade unions and opposition parties are adamant. Even the average citizen loses by not receiving some essential benefits, such as proper streets and sewage, enough school teachers or free medical care for the aged.

That is how things stand now. But we must think about the future. It is widely known that the population is aging rapidly. In fact, by the year 2020, Japan is expected to have the oldest population in the world with more than 20% of the people aged 65 or over. This indicates, without the least doubt, that Japan is going to face tremendous problems of social security, retirement pensions, medical assistance, and so on. It will be in dire need of more hospitals and old age homes as well as the personnel to staff them.

Yet, nothing is being done about that. The administrative reform is largely static and backward-looking. Its sole purpose is to trim costs that exist today, without showing much concern about raising funds that will be needed tomorrow. If anything, rather than prepare the way for a more extensive and supportive social welfare system, it is undermining what little now exists. This, to convert an old saying to the local coin, is "being *sen*-wise and *yen*-foolish."

While no one can object to eliminating waste and increasing the efficiency of the administrative machinery as presently constituted, that should only be one side of the matter. The Ad Hoc Commission has regrettably overlooked the most challenging part of its task by failing to give Japan a government administration that can handle the many problems already appearing on the horizon.

The old age explosion. No population has ever aged faster. Share of population aged 65 and over.

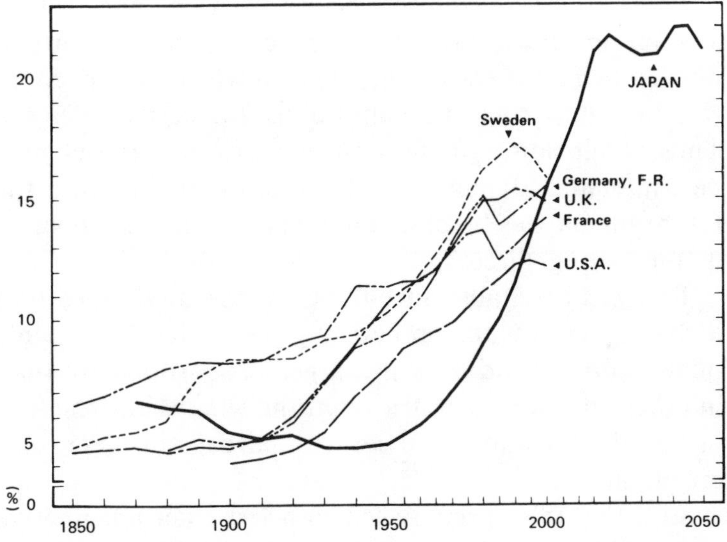

Source: *Survey On people's Living*, Prime Minister's Office, October 1981.

Credit: *'82 Japan* Prime Minister's Office, p.6

Forward-Looking Reforms

In the long succession of administrative reforms, it is already clear that the Doko Commission will be remembered as the most vigorous and most courageous. Its members were tougher and its reports went further than anything that had been seen thus far. For once, there is even a fair chance that some of the recommendations may actually be put into practice.

But there is still no reason to assume that this exercise will leave the country with a much better government administration than it had. For, like its predecessors, the Second Ad Hoc Commission on Administrative Reform was much more concerned with the past than the present or future. Also, packed with representatives of big business, it was much more anxious to save money than anything else.

These are obviously weaknesses in an operation which should, in theory at least, be geared much more to overhauling and renovating a system which, in any country, falls into ruts and fails to rise to new challenges. Thus, while some of the past excesses and abuses may be eliminated, Japan is no better equipped to face the future than it was before. If anything, it has been pointed in the wrong direction.

This was inevitable once the Commission decided that its basic goal was to combat "big government." Japan's public administration is no larger proportionately than in other advanced countries. On the whole, it is smaller, just as the tax and social security burdens of its citizens are lighter.

Still, this false premise led to a less than imaginative attack along two lines: to freeze or shrink government expenditures and, correlated therewith, to freeze or shrink the govenment bureaucracy. The outcome was relatively balanced and across-the-board cuts in both funds and personnel with the sole exception that, in certain ways, education, health and welfare suffered more than most.

Alas, there can be no rational basis for reducing *any* administration uniformly. If cuts are to be made, they should be made where the staff is bloated and funds are wasted. If, to the contrary, newer activities are understaffed and underfunded, they should definitely receive larger allocations. In this sense, a valid administrative reform would have assumed a very different shape.

The first step would have been to choose those areas where reductions are truly justified.

The prime candidate, as everyone already knows, is the Ministry of Agriculture, Forestry and Fisheries which has a huge staff and grants tremendous subsidies. The primary sector is shrinking, the population affected is an ever smaller minority, and these are things for which Japan will never become very competitive. The more resources are mobilized in a desperate attempt to revive the sector, the more are wasted. Rather than launch plans which stand some chance of success, money is squandered to promote (read, subsidize) just about every crop under the sun when it would be wiser to import.

So much was understood by the business leaders who ran the show this time. But they failed to reflect that other ministries in their own bailiwick were not much better. The Ministry of International Trade and Industry, for all its extraordinary reputation, no longer fulfills terribly significant purposes. In the early days of recovery and reconstruction, it played a crucial role. Since then, its influence has not ceased waning as private companies manage to look after their own needs. The only ones which turn to it are the ailing sectors, for whom support is not much more useful than for the farmers. Otherwise, it tries to remain in the limelight by mounting publicity stunts like the fifth generation computer and technopolises.

The Economic Planning Agency is even more anomalous considering that the country no longer engages in economic planning . . . if it ever did. It is hard to justify a regular staff and budget to turn out forecasts and white papers that smack of wishful thinking and are often misleading.

With increasing liberalization, there will be less need for both MITI and EPA. But there will still be a strong need for the Small and Medium Enterprise Agency, a subsidiary of MITI, because this category in the dual economy has never fared well. Smaller firms have less access to funds, more trouble recruiting personnel, and are squeezed by the larger companies many subcontract for. They are the ones facing the biggest difficulties at present. More help for them would be warranted. This could also be promoted by the Fair Trade Commission which, by preventing collusion, could also render considerable service to the consumers.

The Ministry of Posts and Telecommunications, the Ministry of Transport and the Ministry of Construction all perform essentially useful functions. However, since the period of rapid expansion is over, and growth will be slower, there is room for retrenchment. With private railways outperforming the national railways and private delivery services undercutting the post office, there is doubtlessly also room for rationalization.

Finally, while this is the least likely result of any administrative reform, the Ministry of Finance might be cut back. Over the decades, the commercial banks, insurance companies, securities brokers, and so on have developed enough competence to get by on their own. Even formally, most of the regulations have disappeared and the liberalization is bound to continue. This means that there is not that much for the MOF to do aside from worry about the budget deficits and accumulating national bonds.

In all these sectors, it would seem entirely justified to cut both the funds and staff. This would not really prejudice the activities since there would still be enough resources to accomplish the remaining work.

There is one further activity which falls into a strange twilight zone, defense. To judge by the debates, the overweening desire of the government is to boost the defense budget to the detriment of everything else. Yet, a look at the figures will show that the increases are only marginal and Japan has uncommonly low defense expenditures as a share of GNP. This is not said to condone greater spending, nor to condemn it. It is about time that the Japanese realized that defense is not an ordinary item and that the effort should be a function of the nation's political and military stance rather than merely a budgetary issue.

On the other hand, there is a clear and growing need to expand some relatively neglected operations.

Certainly, more should be done not only to protect but also to promote the environment. So far, the primary concern has been to limit pollution and there is still a lot to do in this direction. However, if more thought were given to positive actions, like improving the national parks or planting some greenery in the cities, it would not be amiss. If nothing else, the Environment Agency should be regarded as a national concern and become less subject to the influence of business circles.

With Japan heading toward a "knowledge-intensive" economy, it would be assumed that those dispensing knowledge would enjoy somewhat higher priority. To judge by the shabby and ill-equipped schools and the

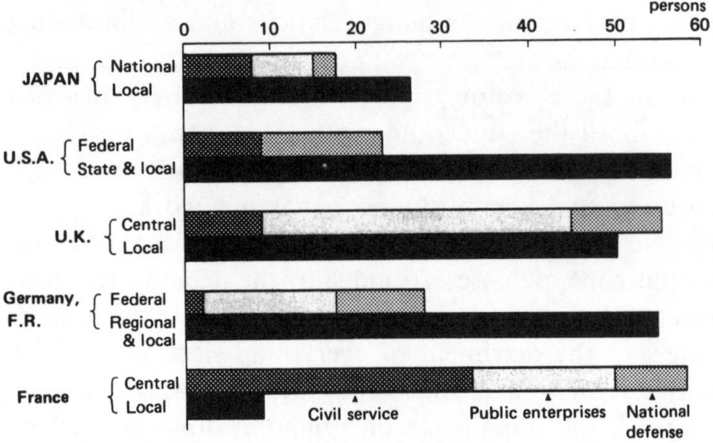

Credit: *'82 Japan*, Prime Minister's Office, p. 71.

shortage of teachers, they do not. A bit of growth in the educational budget, if not necessarily in the Ministry, might help. But this would all be of doubtful benefit if it were not possible to carry out an educational reform that corrects the most crying abuses.

Last, but certainly not least, comes the field of health and welfare. With the population aging rapidly, the number of ill and incapacitated persons increasing by leaps and bounds, and the needs due to continue swelling for another few decades, it would appear obvious that this is the principal sector for growth. If more is not done, the nation could easily plunge into a tragedy of unprecedented proportions. Worse, when the danger is finally perceived, it might be too late to remedy because it is impossible to train staff, build special facilities, and accumulate funds quickly.

Here, as throughout this category, it is preferable to expand the staff in the Ministry of Health and Welfare, or the Ministry of Education, carefully and gradually.

The bulk of the personnel should be allocated to the actual operations, the schools, hospitals, old age homes and so on. The bulk of the money should be directed toward helping people and not creating institutions. With that proviso, it would seem urgent to expand, and expand, and expand ... but certainly not to cut back.

So, rather than a uniform containment or shrinkage of the administration, what is needed is to reshape it fundamentally, reducing some parts, maintaining others, and expanding yet others. While this would not be easy anywhere, it involves special complications in Japan. For, as will become clear during the implementation of the present reform, execution is largely in the hands of the bureaucracy itself.

Still, a more far-reaching and constructive reform of this nature would not be entirely incompatible with its interests. The primary concern is not so much to dismiss employees but to reallocate them, not to deprive them of jobs but to give them more purposeful ones. That is not impossible, although it certainly is difficult. It may just be facilitated by the fact that few bureaucrats are specialists in any particular field but rather generalists who could carry on elsewhere.

Then, once they are installed where the work loads have grown and not where activities have diminished, the administration may run more efficiently than ever. It may just turn out that the number of bureaucrats was not so excessive but that a poor distribution had induced the waste and sloth that were rightly criticized.

Better Now Than Later

To hear them groan, you would think that the Japanese paid the highest taxes in the world and were really crushed by the burden. However, even the most superficial look at the tax situation for people living in countries at roughly the same income levels shows that this is far from true.

The share of taxes of all sorts in national income is much higher in other advanced nations. While Japan's level in 1980 was only 22%, it was 29% in the United States and 32% in Germany. It was a more formidable 37% in Great Britain and as much as 53% in Sweden. The levels in all countries have increased since then, only somewhat more quickly in Japan.

Breaking the tax revenue down into categories, it turns out that the poor Japanese wage-earner is not more put upon than, let's say, the American or British counterpart. A Japanese who is married, with two children, and earning ¥3 million a year (i.e. very close to the typical case) would only pay 3.9% tax. An American in similar conditions would pay 6.3% and a Brit, 19.1%.

Big business has recently complained that it, in fact, is the worst victim of the Japanese tax system. The Federation of Economic Organizations (Keidanren) has provided much circumstantial evidence. The statutory rate is particularly high at 53%. And the alleged real tax burden, at 52%, is much higher than the levels in other countries. In the United States it is only 38%, in France 43% and in Germany 46%.

But this is only meaningful if the corporations actually declare profits. If they break even or make a loss, there is no taxation at all and perhaps some form of relief instead. It is therefore interesting to note that less than half of Japan's incorporated firms claim to be making a profit, and that is usually a rather modest one. The other half are busy making losses.

It is thus rather difficult to pity the poor Japanese taxpayers, whether individual or corporate. If anything, they should be roundly scolded. Not only do they not pay especially high rates given their relative affluence, they have not even mustered enough tax revenue to cover current expenditures. For over a decade, the budget has had to operate through deficit financing and this seems likely to continue another decade or two.

This would appear to be a prima facie case for urging the Japanese to admit the sad facts of life and boost their taxes. If they do not do it bit by bit at present, they will have little choice but to do so massively somewhat later or to accept national bankruptcy.

Obviously, increased taxation is not very appealing. The only one who had the courage to propose it was the late Prime Minister Ohira. When this lost him an election, it became evident that other politicians would only soft-pedal the issue and sneak in minor tax hikes when the occasion permitted. But this sort of puttering about will never solve the nation's ticklish financial problems.

There is a pressing need for a major fiscal reform, one introducing considerable increases in taxation for all categories, as soon as possible. This is fully documented by the studies of the Ministry of Finance or the government's Taxation System Council. It is probably conceded secretly by the opposition as well, although it prefers letting the ruling party brave the popular wrath.

Perhaps what is needed is the general consumption tax that was proposed by Ohira and the Ministry of Finance. Perhaps the tax reform should take another form. That is something that can only be worked out when it is finally admitted that the country cannot continue without major improvements.

However, both in addition to the tax reform and as a temporary solution until then, it would be worthwhile considering how the present fiscal system could bring

Japan's burden is lighter. Percent of taxes, social security and both to national income.

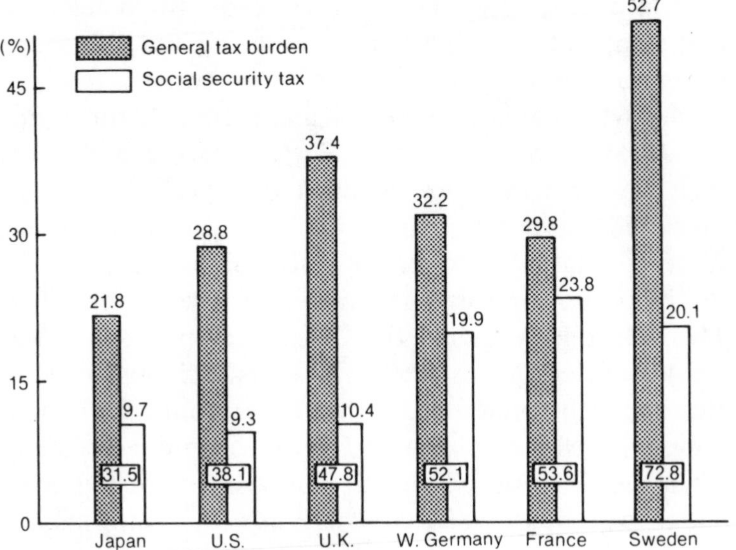

Source: Ministry of Finance
Credit: *Keidanren Review*, October 1980, p. 3.

in more revenue than it does and, in so doing, remove some of the existing inequities.

As noted, the present tax levels for individual wage-earners are not terribly high. But they are clearly imbalanced. Company employees, whose taxes are deducted at the source, have little choice but to declare the actual amount they earned and then petition the tax authorities for any refund they may have a right to.

The situation is completely different for the self-employed. They declare what they want and often fail to include all their earnings. They can also write off many expenses, real or fictitious. Indeed, some have treated their wife, children and even mistress as employees. And it has happened that cars, jewelry or wedding presents would be written off as business expenses.

The worst offenders seem to be the doctors and dentists, many of whom also run clinics and pharmacies. They earn very considerable sums but pay relatively little tax. It is even harder to keep track of the earnings, licit or not, of money-lenders, land speculators, restaurant and hotel owners, or bar and nightclub proprietors. The mass of ordinary shopkeepers apparently pay less than their share and farmers are barely taxed at all even though they are major beneficiaries of government largesse.

The situation is not much better for incorporated firms. As mentioned, about half of them claim to be making no profit. This is partly because small entrepreneurs write off salaries to themselves and relatives as well as less than fully justifiable expenses. But, in addition, many simply dodge taxes by hiding income.

The extent of this is truly amazing. According to the National Tax Administration Agency, one in four firms evaded income taxes. In addition, half of the companies evaded stamp taxes and many kept untaxed income in deposits with banks and other financial institutions.

The amounts involved were tremendous. In 1983, some ¥999 billion in corporate income was found not to have been declared. To this must be added another ¥16 billion in interest or due for stamp taxes. These figures, by the way, only apply to the one-tenth of all companies which were inspected that year. The real amount should be ten times higher or more.

Many of the companies engaged in such practices are quite small and hard to control. In one case, a driving school owner put aside ¥230 million which was used to build a huge mansion, which gave him away and was later dubbed "tax evasion castle." But the big companies are sometime worse, according to the National Tax Administration Agency. Those evading taxes included some of the supposed elite of the corporate world, such as

Mitsui which failed to declare ¥3.6 billion, Marubeni which forgot to mention ¥10 billion, and Mitsubishi which overlooked ¥11 billion, and later another ¥5.9 billion.

If most of these tax loopholes could be closed, it would be possible to net much tax revenue without increasing the rates. If the National Tax Administration Agency would take on more inspectors, it could doubtlessly uncover much more tax evasion, enough to pay for the additional personnel and then add substantially to the government's kitty. But, most important, if the tax system seemed fairer and more efficient, the general public might be more willing to accept a proper tax reform.

The situation for social security and health insurance is in some ways similar. Japanese workers are not surprisingly annoyed to have to fork out 10% of their wages (half from the employee, half from the employer) for social security. Then comes another 8% or so for health insurance. This is an awful lot of money. But it is still considerably less than Western workers have to pay for their schemes. More to the point, even now it is inadequate to cover the disbursements which means that any shortfalls must be met by the national budget.

What then would the Japanese workers think about doubling the percentages? Certainly nothing printable. Yet, there are more than enough studies and statistics to show that this will be necessary by the end of the century or shortly thereafter. The alternative is to continue dismantling the present system as less and less is provided. This is probably the way Japan will go unless there is an unexpected awareness of the gravity of the situation.

But running down the health and welfare system will not really help. It will only signify that, rather than paying the costs out of a broader fund, individuals will have to pay separately. So, the costs will not be smaller. In fact, they are likely to be larger since the efforts will be dispersed. What is more serious, however, is that by shifting the burden to the individual the principal advantage of any mutual arrangement will be lost. Rather than everyone pooling resources to help those who due to some misfortune are in need, it will be each person, or each family, for itself. And some are bound not to have the wherewithal.

Here, too, it would be far wiser to pay now than later. It will be roughly the same amount of money in the end. But the effort will be less painful by spreading it over more time and more people. As with taxes, it would doubtlessly also be easier to convince the public of the need if the government made a frank and clear presentation of the state of affairs and proposed a system that might be broadly acceptable. That is certainly better than patching up health and social security schemes that are known to be untenable and increasingly insolvent.

So, instead of feeling sorry for themselves, the Japanese people might admit that paying more taxes and higher welfare premiums is an inevitable fact of life. It is one that has been accepted, without particularly liking it, in many other countries. Moreover, when the time comes to benefit, the effort will prove to have been more than worth it. Meanwhile, they might also send a message to the political leadership that the government cannot keep its head in the sand either. The bills will have to be paid!

12
Setting New goals

Why Wait For The 21st Century?

The time is early 1984. The place is the Japanese National Diet. Prime Minister Yasuhiro Nakasone is making his policy speech outlining the nation's future program.

Yet, although the year is 1984, half of the speech is devoted to the 21st century. That is apparently the time when Japan will finally come into its own. That is the time when the Japanese people will live in "warmly personal communities of solidarity and culture," when they can enjoy "safe and comfortable residential environments bedecked with flowers and greenery." Going beyond that, he even speaks of "creating a society which, in addition to its material affluence, treasures the sublimity of man's spirit, has a respect for civility and the other person, maintains its unity, and wins the respect of the world's peoples."

That is the world of the 21st century toward which the Japanese must strive and for which they must make the necessary sacrifices. And sacrifices there will be. For the other half of his speech indicates the measures that must be adopted to lay the foundations for the 21st century. They include, first and foremost, both an administrative and a fiscal reform. In short, as the audience already knows, the citizenry will have to expect less from the government yet pay more for it. Thus, to reach this wonderful future world, it is essential for the Japanese people to "maintain their diligence."

But Nakasone leaves his public with a ray of hope: "I know that times are difficult. Yet a brighter future lies ahead. I see in the distance a vision of Japan as a richly verdant Pacific archipelago off the east coast of Asia, the home of a new culture integrating the best of East and West."

While it may seem strange for a country which is generally regarded as highly developed and affluent to be told that everything should be endured for a better world that will only emerge in some twenty years or more, this has already become commonplace in Japan. For,

Mt. Fuji with factories. Isn't it about time for a new image?

Credit: Jon Woronoff

before Nakasone, Prime Ministers Fukuda, Ohira, and Suzuki also called upon the people to prepare for the 21st century. They also promised rich and agreeable lives, occasionally embellished with visions of "regional plazas" or "pastoral cities."

And, just like Nakasone, they offered precious little in the way of comfort for the present. Rather than shorten working hours, efforts were made to have people work a few years longer. Rather than see that workers took vacations or saw their families, they let companies pressure them into spending even their supposedly free time at work. Rather than putting more funds into housing, amenities or social overhead, they gave precedence to investment in plant and equipment. Rather than actively creating solid health and social security systems, they began taking apart the rather skimpy ones that existed.

For, as seems to befit the Japanese spirit, they felt that the times were difficult. The times were always difficult for Japan one way or the other. And the only way of overcoming whatever crisis there happened to be was to postpone the day of reward and fulfillment another few years and meanwhile accept any necessary sacrifices. The Japanese should continue scrimping and saving, showing their devotion and work ethic, and refrain from making excessive demands for present gratification.

All that is hardly new. During the 1950s, the Japanese were told to pull in their belts in order to rebuild the economy. During the 1960s, they had to forget their personal desires and throw all their efforts into expanding industry and exporting. As compensation, the politicians already started promising that in another decade or so they should enjoy better living conditions and a superior lifestyle. Alas, in the 1970s, after the setbacks of the oil shocks and protectionism, they were again asked to forget the present and work for a greater, more distant future.

Japanese economic development has truly been a miracle of postponed rewards, of present deprivation to build a better world of the future. Few peoples have shown as much discipline in using today's wealth to invest in tomorrow's production, in accepting that more factories and machinery were needed and that better housing or more leisure would have to be foregone in the interim. Yet, when the great day of fulfillment is postponed beyond the year 2000, it is certainly time to say "enough!"

It is natural to suffer after losing a war. It is normal to plow everything back into production when the economy is small and fragile. But such an approach makes no sense for a country which proudly boasts of producing 10% of world GNP and manages to crush its competitors under massive exports. It makes no sense that people with comparatively high income levels should continue living in rabbit hutches with few amenities or parks and gardens while behaving like workaholics with little time to engage in personal or family activities.

All about Japan there are countries which have accepted that sacrifice has to be balanced with reward, that one should work today but also do some enjoying now as well. In the West, just about every country offers its people much more vacation and free time. Just about every country has put more stress on better housing and some concern for a more attractive environment. Just about every country recognizes social security and welfare as valid expenses. When they sacrifice, it is often to make life more worth living rather than less.

This happens not only in the advanced nations. In poorer East Asian countries like Hong Kong and Taiwan, people work extremely hard during the day, frequently outdoing the Japanese. But they make up for it by seeing their friends and family, enjoying entertainment or eating out together, something few Japanese salarymen are permitted. Singapore, with a much lower income level, is already a garden city such as Japan will probably never become.

The primary explanation is not the relative wealth or lack of problems, for they are sometimes poorer and usually face more difficulties, but the way in which priorities are ordered. As long as improvements in personal life and living conditions are relegated to the next decade, or the next century, that is when the improvements will come. As long as people can be persuaded to sacrifice today in the vain hope of some reward tomorrow, the reward will not come any sooner.

What aspects of daily life are most important to you? The priorities are clear.

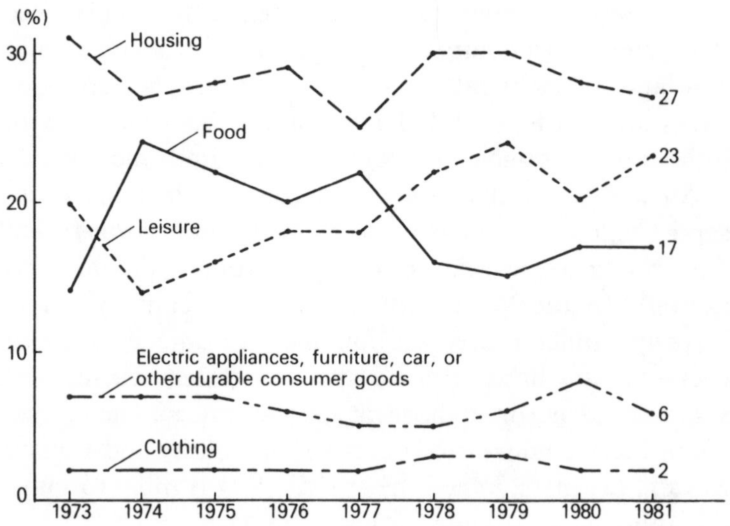

Source: *Survey On People's Living*, Prime Minister's Office, October 1981.
Credit: *Facts & Figures 1982*, Foreign Press Center, p. 154.

Since there is little chance that the government will change its approach, any changes must come from the population. It is high time that the Japanese ceased accepting everything the government decides and expressed more clearly what they want of society. It is time to call for more, not less, spending on social overhead, education and housing, health insurance and social security. It is time to notify employers that wages can be raised, perhaps by buying less machinery, and that the best response to sluggish sales is not to work harder but a little less.

If the priorities are not altered, the situation will continue in the future as it was in the past. Sacrifice today for rewards which are not only postponed but repeatedly put off for much later. Dreams of a millenium which never comes. However, if the Japanese finally impose their will on the government and employers, they could enjoy a much better life without having to wait until the 21st century.

Time To Grow Up

With each passing year, the Japanese leadership is more worried about catching what it regards as the worst possible social ailment, namely the "advanced nation disease." The contagion has been spreading rapidly. It originated in England and was once assumed to be contained there, for which reason it was initially called the "English disease." But it spread across the Channel and attacked one European country after the other, including even the once immune Germany. The United States and Canada also fell victims. The only advanced nation that apparently managed to escape it was Japan.

Just what this disease consisted of was not so easy to explain. Symptoms varied with the patients just as diagnoses varied with the physicians. But there was a general agreement on certain basic characteristics.

Most noticeable was a loss of work will. People ceased putting in long hours at work and, while on the job, they also ceased working as hard. Leisure became more important than work and jobs had to be made "fun" to even attract employees. This was further exacerbated by unruly trade unions. The results were evident. Productivity stagnated and sometimes fell. Economic growth became sluggish.

But this was not all. Although people were working less, they were constantly demanding more. The unemployed, without even working, insisted on being paid for extended periods, and paid at rates very close to normal wages. The number of ill increased dramatically, medical and hospital bills mounted, and more of the nation's wealth was tied up in caring for the aged. Social security expenditures expanded at a rapid clip. That, at least, was for those who had put aside some of their own money. Worse was the growing need to provide welfare for others.

More serious, clear signs of decadence abounded. Crime and juvenile delinquency spread and the cities became unsafe. Young people engaged in bizarre individualistic extravagances and sometimes anti-social acts. Society's basic rules were flaunted and national solidarity undermined. The population became troublesome and, in some segments, almost unmanageable.

Naturally, these problems had unwelcome financial implications. Wage costs plus fringe benefits, including an increasing number of "frills," snowballed. Expenditures for unemployment, health care, social security, public welfare, and so on skyrocketed. Taxes kept swelling and became a heavy burden.

This was clearly a disease that many Japanese in positions of authority, especially in the business world, did not want to catch. They therefore reacted by stressing Japan's time-honored traditions and inculcating its ancient virtues. They also bore down on the working population by imposing relatively long hours for relatively modest remuneration and treating union calls for more free time and bigger wage hikes as unpatriotic. Meanwhile, every effort was made to cut back on the government administration and prune the still quite rudimentary medical care and social welfare systems.

But it was impossible to halt the advance of this awful affliction. Like it or not, many of the causes were inherent in the maturing of any economy and aging of any society. Certain phenomena were bound to arise no matter what one wanted and no matter what one did.

One notable cause of the "advanced nation disease" is the increase in the number of old people. They can hardly be blamed for getting older. Nor is it really their fault if they should need more medical care and hospitalization. It is equally unavoidable that many of them, ill or simply aged, should have to cease working and be looked after by the state. The more a population ages, the more such people there will be. In Japan, this trend will be more rapid and pronounced than anywhere else.

Other aspects can be traced to the slowdown of the economy. In even the most dynamic economy, there must come a time when little more growth can be attained. Also, in advanced economies, more of the production comes from use of machinery and less from labor of people. As agriculture, then industry, and ultimately services, mature and either decline or become less labor-intensive, there will be more and more people who simply cannot find work. Others, for one reason or another, will not really need to work.

Finally, just as inevitable a cause as the rest, there is an evolution in the mentalities as one generation follows another. Those growing up in a poor society, where one must work to survive, are bound to have a different work ethic from their children or grandchildren who were born into a society which is reasonably affluent and where one tends to select the kind of work one wants. Living in a more democratic, more egalitarian society, youngsters will not so readily accept the views of their elders and will experiment with their own lifestyles.

This is hardly decadence. But it may create a suitable environment if not carefully handled. Unemployed people, those who cannot make ends meet otherwise, would be more tempted either to drop out or engage in antisocial behavior. Young people who find that old notions and practices are hopelessly out of place will be less willing to accept orders from above. With a bit more money of their own, they may also find dubious manners of spending it. It is not surprising that, even in Japan, there should have been some increase in crime and delinquency, divorce, drug addiction, pornography and prostitution, and so on.

Since these phenomena are going to emerge in Japan no matter what it does, it would be wisest to consider how they were dealt with in the West. As for every earlier stage in its development, Japan, as a late-comer, has the tremendous advantage of seeing what was done by others so as to select the smarter solutions and avoid the foolish ones. In this case, it might do well to consider that most of the measures were actually quite rational but only went wrong when they were overdone. By avoiding excesses, Japan could once again improve on its teachers.

If people are going to age, then retire and need pensions, fall ill and need medical care or hospitalization,

How do you want your working environment improved? The priorities are clear again.

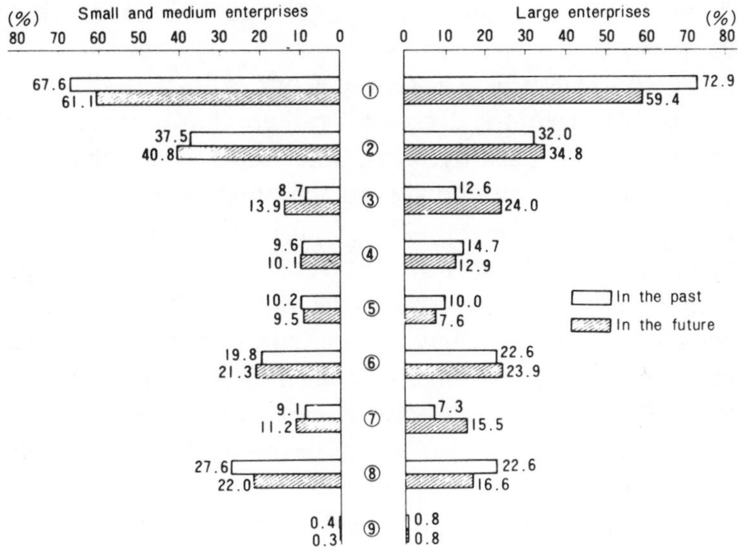

①Increase in wages
②Shortening of working hours(including implementation of the five-day workweek system, acquisition of long vacations and other actions for increasing days off and vacations)
③Promotion to more responsible, more authoritative positions;
④Securing of educational and research opportunities
⑤Improvement and full development of the working environment, such as emphasis on labor safety and hygiene;
⑥Improving and enlarging company benefits
⑦Opportunity for making suggestions (proposals) on management policies;
⑧Emphasis on a pleasant, enjoyable place of work atmosphere;
⑨Other

Source: *Survey on Consciousness of Workers*, Small and Medium Enterprise Agency, November 1979.
Credit: *While Paper on Small and Medium Enterprise 1980*, MITI, p. 43.

denying this will not help. It is essential to build the basic infrastructure, the clinics, hospitals, old age homes and so on while putting aside the necessary funds. The amount of money needed can be calculated according to standard actuarial procedures. One can, of course, try to limit the more extravagant medical equipment and treatment and have old age homes that are comfortable but not luxurious. Unemployment and social security benefits may be kept somewhat lower than in, say, Scandinavia. But certainly much more has to be done than at present.

As concerns the weakening work will, actually it is probably wiser to decrease—rather than increase or maintain—the existing work schedules. It will become ever more necessary to spread the amount of work that exists among those capable of performing it. This may result in considerably more free time for everybody, which could also undermine the work ethic, but that is certainly better than having sub-cultures of unemployed or unemployable persons. As for an expectation of higher wages, if the cost of living rises or the company does well, it is rather hard to explain to the staff why it should not want more.

There are also bound to be changes in lifestyles. Most of them will probably be more relaxed and individualistic. Trying to suppress them or pushing the old samurai ethic, as illustrated by Toshiwo Doko, just won't work. It would be much wiser to educate people in the intelligent use of their expanding free time. This could improve the educational and cultural level or promote more social awareness and community service. Even if some of it is wasted, there is not much to fear in giving the Japanese a bit more leisure.

Indeed, this might do more to improve society and avoid decadence than anything else. Many of Japan's social problems arise because the parents (especially fathers) do not spend enough time with their children. More free time would permit this and go much further by providing useful adult models. Even if they are not traditionally Japanese, the rising generations' my-home and new-family ideologies are hardly subversive.

Thus, the best way to avoid a serious case of the "advanced country disease'' is probably to accept a small, and carefully controlled dose, much in the form of a vaccination. Then even greater doses could be tolerated without excessive danger although, as the elders fear, one must avoid going too far.

To reject this makes little sense. To look back and say that, in the olden days, we had none of these things so we don't need them now is hardly relevant. So much has changed since those bygone days. To say that this was once a problem of the family does not help any more. The present-day nuclear family has little in common with the traditional extended family. To say that the Japanese spirit will prevail would be an even more notable blunder. No spirit can make up for a lack of facilities, personnel and funds.

Moreover, any other policy would be considerably worse. Refusing to accept the maturing of the economy and aging of the population would be unrealistic. It would make Japan look increasingly silly, applying old solutions to new problems or making believe that the problems don't exist. For those most directly concerned, it would be worse than ridiculous. It would be terribly cruel to punish them for losing their job, falling ill, or just growing old.

If Japan could adopt Western technologies, if it could introduce alien ideas and cultures, if it could construct a modern economy, then certainly it can take the additional step of fashioning a social policy that fits its present status as an advanced nation. If it were to fail here, then most of its past successes would be of little value. And it would probably fare even worse than those it criticizes for succumbing to the ''advanced nation disease.''

Promoting Net National Well-Being

A bit over a decade ago, one of the prime minister's many advisory committees came up with an idea which, although long since forgotten, is certainly worth recalling. This is the concept of net national welfare which was to be opposed to the recognized concept of gross national product that had been the primary goal of Japan's economic activities ever since the war.

Not surprisingly, the NNW Development Committee, a minor organ of the Economic Deliberation Council, went about its work with a typical meticulousness and lack of imagination. It painstakingly drew up lists of items which were not included in GNP and should be added to or substracted from it to attain NNW, and then gave the value, growth rate, and gap between the two down to the last yen.

Alas, its report was submitted early in 1973 and, not long after, the country was engulfed in the first oil crisis which quickly turned its thoughts from welfare back to production. The obsession with production, and neglect of welfare, has therefore continued another decade and bides well to remain with Japan until its people finally realize that NNW is certainly at least as valid a goal as GNP.

This makes it more vital than ever to take another look at the idea and see what it does offer in the way of alternative growth strategies. In so going, the approach will be less mechanistic than that of the NNW Development Committee and the concept will be broadened to net national well-being, since welfare has a specific content and does not begin to cover the many things that could, and should, be done to make Japan a more pleasant and livable place.

First of all, as must be obvious, there are items which

go into GNP but actually diminish NNW. They are the more unfortunate consequences of an unbridled development policy that induces external diseconomies.

The quickest, although hardly wisest, way to boost output is to mine or import masses of raw material, process them in huge plants and turn out endless series of standardized products. Factories will be large, concentrated, and run full blast. There will be little time or money devoted to keeping operations clean or safe. People will move to the source of work as bedroom towns emerge to receive them. Forests will be torn down and hills levelled to make way for civilization.

This is excellent for production. But it harms well-being. There is bound to be considerable pollution, cities will become overcrowded in some parts while population sinks in others, and people will be working too much to look after other, equally important concerns, like raising children or engaging in community activities. There will be housing, but little else of what is needed for a true neighborhood. And nature will be a remote and diminishing residual.

There are also many things that go into GNP but do not contribute directly to NNW. The items which defenders of growth at all costs prefer naturally derive from private investment in plant and equipment. They consist of more mines, more factories, more power plants, more machinery, more robots and computers and so on. This gives a direct boost to production and keeps the industrial sector booming.

It also helps NNW indirectly. The wealth generated through these activities can be channeled into the other basic category of investment, social overhead. This includes schools and hospitals, water supply and sewage disposal, parks and playgrounds, etc. These things most definitely contribute to well-being, and very directly, but they only seem a pitiful waste to the GNP fanatics.

In an export-oriented economy, this distinction assumes even greater significance. For it requires an immediate investment in plant and equipment, an investment which becomes much larger than if the country were less concerned with exporting. Once the exports are sold, some of that money can also be channeled into domestic social overhead. But it takes somewhat longer for it to get there.

Finally, there are a number of things which detract from GNP but contribute very substantially to NNW.

One of them can be summed up as welfare. It includes things like medical treatment, old age care, social security, and the many facilities and masses of personnel that go with them. That is not to say that they do not contribute to GNP in their own way, since doctors' or social workers' remuneration will also be recorded. But they

A rare glimpse of happy old age. Perhaps everybody can play some day.

Credit: Foreign Press Center/Kyodo

are not as productive as a factory or power plant in generating more growth.

The other basic category here is leisure. If people work fewer hours, there is no doubt that there will be some reduction in productive output. This may bear heavily on the companies which probably have to pay more proportionately for each hour worked. This explains why leisure is not much appreciated by the proponents of GNP. Yet, once again, leisure is the basis of an industry which makes its contribution to the economy.

This is probably also the place to mention a host of other things which are essentially "free," although presently out of reach for many Japanese. Take, for example, the opportunity to enjoy the company of one's friends or relatives, to go for a walk in the city or coutryside for the pure pleasure of doing so, to read poetry or listen to music if that is what one fancies. It even includes things like falling in love, setting off on an adventure, and improving oneself physically or spiritually. These are things which may never be recorded in the national accounts of well-being, but should certainly not be overlooked.

While welfare, leisure and pleasure are not very helpful when it comes to boosting production, they are incredibly precious in improving the lifestyle of the population. And that is more than enough reason to give then an appropriate weight in any evaulation of economic progress. This is even more justified for advanced economies, like that of present-day Japan, than developing ones, such as it used to be.

Thus, net national well-being is a perfectly valid indicator, in no way inferior to gross national product, if one wishes to measure the benefits that flow from an economy. It is a yardstick not of how productive an economy is but rather how fruitful. It is probably the ideal indicator for those who wish to know what they are getting out as opposed to what they are putting in.

Once such conclusions are drawn, and they probably have been reached in some nebulous form by most Japanese, it is necessary to think of implementation. Knowing what contributes most significantly to NNW, it is easy enough to promote those things directly or indirectly.

It is possible to improve the environment in various ways. Stricter limits on truck exhaust or disposal of specific pollutants can be introduced, something which is sorely needed to save the nation's lakes and rivers. More positively, programs can be launched to clean up some of the mess, to build parks and gardens, to create wild life preserves and national parks, and to promote a love of nature.

To enhance personal living conditions, more could be done to provide amenities, spreading the networks of tap water, flush toilets, sewage and so on. Proper housing, of adequate size and reasonable comfort, could also be constructed. More generally, by introducing appropriate zoning laws it would be easier to create decent and perhaps even attractive residential districts. If the growth of major cities, especially Tokyo, could be controlled and some institutions moved out, there would be less crowding.

Leisure could certainly be increased as regards the amount of free time. Full weekends, shorter working hours (and less overtime), as well as longer vacations, could finally be adopted. Moreover, to see that they are applied, the govenment could make these improvements legally enforceable and issue very strong administrative guidance to smooth the way.

Finally, money could be set aside for health insurance, old age pensions, social security and so on. Meanwhile, the necessary facilities (hospitals, old age homes, etc.) could be built and the essential personnel (doctors, geriatrists, social workers, etc.) trained. This would meet many of the specific needs and also relieve much of the anguish of not knowing how one will get by.

Some of this, amazingly enough, would cost relatively little, such as improved housing, intelligent zoning and more free time. The rest would involve greater expenses, including most amenities, while social security and health care would amount to rather large sums. But all of it would certainly be more than worth the money.

What is necessary is for the Japanese people to reconsider the options. Do they really want another ten, twenty or thirty years of the mad race for more output? Or are they ready to slow down and create a more comfortable life for themselves? If it were finally possible to impose NNW as an acceptable goal, then the Japanese could truly benefit from their decades of effort.

Bibliography

Baranson, Jack, *The Japanese Challenge to U.S. Industry,* Lexington, D.C. Heath, 1981.

Barnds, William J. (ed.), *Japan and the United States, Challenges & Opportunities*, New York University Press, 1979.

Bronte, Stephen, *Japanese Finance: Markets and Institutions,* London, Euromoney, 1982.

Davidson, William H., *The Amazing Race: Winning the Technorivalry with Japan,* New York, John Wiley, 1984.

Destler, I.M., and Sato, Hideo (ed.), *Coping with U.S.-Japanese Economic Conflicts,* Lexington, D.C. Heath, 1982.

Fukutake, Tadashi, *Japanese Society Today,* Tokyo, University of Tokyo Press, 1981.

——, *The Japanese Social Structure,* Tokyo, University of Tokyo Press, 1982.

Hanami, Tadashi, *Labor Relations in Japan Today,* Tokyo, Kodansha, 1979.

Hollerman, Leon (ed.), *Japan and the United States: Economic and Political Adversaries,* Boulder, Westview, 1980.

Kamata, Satoshi, *Japan in the Passing Lane,* New York, Pantheon Books, 1982.

Kosai, Yutaka, and Ogino, Yoshitaro, *The Contemporary Japanese Economy*, Armonk, M.E. Sharpe, 1983.

Levine, Solomon B., and Kawada, Hisashi, *Human Resources in Japanese Industrial Development,* Princeton, Princeton University Press, 1980.

Ministry of International Trade and Industry, *White Paper on International Trade,* Tokyo, various.

Nakamura, Takafusa, *The Postwar Japanese Economy,* Tokyo, University Press, 1981.

Okimoto, Daniel I., Sugano, Takuo, and Weinstein, Franklin B. (ed.), *Competitive Edge, The Semiconductor Industry in the U.S. and Japan,* Stanford, Stanford University Press, 1984.

Schlossstein, Steven, *Trade War*, New York, Congdon & Weed, 1984.

Shinohara, Miyohei, *Industrial Growth, Trade, and Dynamic Patterns in the Japanese Economy,* Tokyo, University of Tokyo Press, 1982.

Shirai, Taishiro (ed.). *Contemporary Industrial Relations in Japan,* Madison, University of Wisconsin Press, 1983.

Shiratori, Rei, *Japan in the 1980s,* Tokyo, Kodansha, 1982.

Small and Medium Enterprise Agency, *White Paper on Small and Medium Enterprises in Japan,* Tokyo, various.

Steven, Rob, *Classes in Contemporary Japan,* Cambridge, Cambridge University Press, 1983.

Uchino, Tatsuro, *Japan's Postwar Economy,* Tokyo, Kodansha, 1983.

Wolf, Marvin J., *The Japanese Conspiracy,* New York, Empire Books, 1983.

Woronoff, Jon, *Inside Japan, Inc.,* Tokyo, Lotus Press, 1982.

——, *Japan's Commercial Empire,* Tokyo, Lotus Press, London, Macmillan, and Armonk, M.E. Sharpe, 1984.

——, *Japan's Wasted Workers,* Tokyo, Lotus Press, and Totowa, Rowman & Allenheld, 1983.

——, *Japan: The Coming Economic Crisis,* Tokyo, Lotus Press, 1979.

——, *Japan: The Coming Social Crisis,* Tokyo, Lotus Press, 1980.

——, *World Trade War,* Tokyo, Lotus Press, and New York, Praeger, 1984.

Yamamura, Kozo (ed.), *Policy and Trade Issues of the Japanese Economy,* Seattle, University of Washington Press, 1982.

Index